Excel Workbook

for

Practical Business Math Procedures

Tenth Edition

Jeffrey Slater
North Shore Community College

Prepared by
Jeff S. Hong
City University of New York

**McGraw-Hill
Irwin**

**McGraw-Hill
Irwin**

Excel Workbook for
PRACTICAL BUSINESS MATH PROCEDURES
Jeffrey Slater

Published by McGraw-Hill/Irwin, an imprint of The McGraw-Hill Companies, Inc., 1221 Avenue of the
Americas, New York, NY 10020. Copyright © 2011, 2008, 2006, 2003, 2000, 1997, 1994, 1991, 1987, 1983 by The
McGraw-Hill Companies, Inc. All rights reserved.

1 2 3 4 5 6 7 8 9 0 WDD/WDD 1 0 9 8 7 6 5 4 3 2 1 0

ISBN: 978-0-07-732790-3
MHID: 0-07-732790-X

www.mhhe.com

Preface

This Excel workbook supports <u>Practical Business Math Procedures</u> (10th Edition) by Jeffrey Slater. The workbook contains problems taken from Chapter 4 through Chapter 22 offering students an opportunity to create their own spreadsheets to solve chapter problems. The goal is to have students learn how a spreadsheet can be used to solve various problems.

In addition this package includes a set of exercises students may use to help with learning the material in each chapter. There are also two problems taken from the problem section at the end of each chapter.

See <u>Appendix B</u> for details.

PART I. You may want to review how to use Excel before you begin this workbook or use the templates. The first section of this workbook explains how to use an Excel spreadsheet. If you have little or no experience with Excel, it is recommended that you do this section before beginning the workbook or using the CD.

PART II. The second section provides students with a problem to solve from chapters 4 through 18 (excluding chapter 5). There are step by step directions to follow but these are only suggestions as there are many ways to use Excel to solve a problem. The formulas used for the text book problems are located in the back of this workbook in <u>Appendix A</u>. You may use the included problems as a supplement when working with the text book or as a review.

After you finish working with the problems you can save them to your disk and/or print them out. Students should have your own storage device – disk, flash drive… etc. It is suggested that you use the chapter number as the file name. For example, after you finish the problems in Chapter 4 you can name the file "C4", and Chapter 6 would be "C6", etc. Be sure to use a NEW NAME before saving a completed worksheet.

PART III. This section contains the learning exercises and the problems taken from the end of each chapter. You will find the information about these in <u>Appendix B</u>. Do not be concerned about the format of the spreadsheet as built in formulas will give strange answers when the yellow information cells are blank. The formulas will compute when you enter the proper data.

Dedication

This book is dedicated to my bundle of joy, Nicole, who has been my sole inspiration and pride from the moment she came into this world.

TABLE OF CONTENTS

Overview of Excel

The Excel spreadsheet is made up of **columns** and **rows**. Each column is headed by a letter of the alphabet and each row is headed by a number. Data is entered where the column and row intersect. This is referred to as a **cell**. When using the spreadsheet, the cell is assigned an "address" which is the column letter followed by the row number. As you move around the spreadsheet, you will see the cell location displayed just above the column letters on the left side of the screen. A black border surrounds the active cell. You can move to any cell address by clicking the mouse pointer in a cell or by using arrow keys. Remember: <u>you must always enter the column number before the row number</u>. B2, C5l, T132 are correct cell addresses; 6lG, 5R, A4A are not correct cell addresses. In the picture below the cell pointer is in A1.

Looking at the Excel screen you will see the following layout:

1) The first row is a menu bar with pull down menus: file, edit, view, insert, format, tools, data, window, and help.

File Edit View Insert Format Tools Data Window Help

2) The next two rows are toolbars with various symbols. If you place the mouse arrow on any of the symbols a "label balloon" appears to indicate what that symbol represents. We will use the CURRENCY Symbol, PERCENT symbol, the INCREASE DECIMAL and DECREASE DECIMAL the most.

CURRENCY   PERCENT   INCREASE   DECREASE

X Microsoft Excel - Book1

File Edit View Insert Format Tools Data Window Help

Courier New   10   B I U $ % , .00 .0   A

A1   =

A   B   C   D   E   F   G   H   I

3) The fourth row is the formula bar, which includes the cell address, and a blank space where data and formula are displayed as you enter them.

A1   =

4) At the bottom of the screen there are two rows. The top row is the area for the sheet names, referred to as "sheet" tabs, and horizontal scroll bar which allows you to move the spreadsheet to the left or right. The last row at the bottom is the status bar.

Sheet1 / Sheet2 / Sheet3 / Sheet4 /

Ready   NUM

5) On the right side of the screen is the vertical scroll bar that allows you to move the spreadsheet up and down.

The active cell, the cell where data is entered, is outlined with a black box. In the lower right side of that box there is an equal sign or a small square dot (this equal sign allows you to copy information from the active cell to other cells by using the mouse). You will notice that the column letter and row number are in bold.

A

1

The mouse pointer is a large plus sign. As you move the mouse pointer to the menu bar or tool bars the large plus sign will change to a white arrow.

When entering data you first choose the cell you wish. You can use either the arrow keys on your keyboard to move in any direction or place the mouse pointer in the cell and click the left mouse button one time. The active cell will have the black box. You may then type either words, called labels, or numbers, called values. The words must fit into the cell or else they will spill over into the adjoining cell (if the adjoining cell is not empty then only a part of the label will be visible). When entering a value there is no spill over available and you will get an error message (a series of ##### symbols will appear). The method to widen the cells is explained later.

In general you will be able to work with the columns and rows that are visible on screen. This will usually be 19 rows and 9 columns. Your spreadsheet, depending on how it was installed, may display an additional of fewer columns and rows. If you need more space use your arrow keys to reach the cells that are not visible.

Once you have chosen the cell you wish to use, you type the information. The data will appear in two places on the screen: in the cell you chose and in the formula bar directly above the column letters. That formula bar gives you the opportunity to make corrections by using the backspace key and retyping data. After you type the data you will note three additional symbols will appear to the left of the data in the formula bar. The first is a red letter X which allows you to cancel what you have done; the second is a green check mark which allows you to enter information onto the spreadsheet; and the third consists of two black letters, an F and an X, which allows you to use a function wizard or built in formula. Data can be entered either in all upper case, all lower case, or a combination.

If the data is correct you proceed by either clicking on the green check mark in the formula bar or by pressing the ENTER key on your keyboard. You then move to the next cell and repeat the operation. If you find you made a mistake, or wish to change your data, just return to the cell and press the DELETE key on your keyboard. That will empty the cell. It is recommended that you place your labels in row one and column A and place your values in a column format. With Excel, you can add, subtract, multiply, or divide in any direction however.

To create a formula use the equal (=) sign followed by the specific math operations you wish. On a spreadsheet you may use numbers in your formulas but it is recommended that you enter the address of the cells that contain the numbers. This allows you to change numbers without having to change the formulas. The symbols you use for mathematical operations are: the plus sign (+) for addition; the minus sign (-) for subtraction; the asterisk symbol (*) for multiplication; and the slash or slant sign (/) for division. In addition you can add a column or row using a built in formula called SUM. The format you will use is as follows:

1) To add a value in cell A2 to a value in A3 you would make cell A4 the active cell. You would then type the equal sign, followed by the cell address of A2, followed by the plus sign, followed by the cell address of A3, and press enter or click the green check mark symbol in the formula bar.

   =A2+A3 (note there are NO SPACES between any parts of the formula).

2) To multiply a value in cell C5 times a value in T6 you would use the following:

   =C5*T6 (note that you use the equal sign no matter what operation you are doing)

3) To add D4 to G6 and subtract R7 you would use the following:

   =D4+G6-R7

You must be careful when building formulas to remember this rule: a spreadsheet will multiply and/or divide BEFORE it will add and/or subtract. In order to reverse that process you must use parenthesis around the part of the formula you wish Excel to do first. Here are examples of the difference when using parenthesis:

A4 has a value of 8, B5 has a value of 2, and C6 has a value of 3.

=A4+B5*C6 will give you a total of 14. (2 times 3 are 6; plus 8 are 14).

=(A4+B5)*C6 will give you a total of 30 (8 plus 2 is 10; times 3 is 30).

When entering labels or values you may need to make the cell wider (the default or basic setting of a cell is 9 spaces wide). You cannot make just one cell wider - you must make the entire column wider. One way to do this is to place the cell pointer on the LETTER of the column and move the pointer to the RIGHT. When you reach the black vertical line that separates the columns the cell pointer will change from a white arrow to a vertical line with a thin black arrow pointing to the left and pointing to the right. Hold the left mouse button down and drag the mouse to the RIGHT. You will see the line that creates the cell edge move to the right. When the entire label or value is inside the cell just let go of the mouse button. The column is now wide enough.

You may also widen a column using the FORMAT menu. Place the mouse arrow on the word FORMAT and click the left mouse button. Next drag the left mouse button on the word COLUMN. You change the column by using the AUTOFIT choice using the left mouse button.

FORMAT   COLUMN   AUTOFIT SELECTION

Try this exercise:

1. Start by loading Excel by double clicking on the Excel icon from the Excel work group or the Microsoft Office work group.
2) Place the cell pointer (white plus sign) into cell B5 and click the left mouse button. The black box should appear to surround cell B5.
3) Type the label "TESTING" into that cell. You can either click on the green check mark or press the ENTER key.
4) Move to cell B6 (if you clicked on the green check mark you now can either place the cell pointer in B6 and click once or press the down arrow key once. If you used the ENTER key you should already be in B6).
5) Type the value 4 and enter it.
6) Move to Cell B7.
7) Type the value 5 and enter it.
8) Move to cell B8. To add those values type the formula: =B6+B7 and enter it. You should get the total of 9.
9) Move to cell C1 and enter the value 6.

10) Move to cell C2 and enter the value 7.
11) Move to cell C3 and type the formula to multiply those values. You should get the total of 42. (That formula should be =C1*C2.)
12) Move to cell D6 and here we will add the values in B6 and B7 and then multiple times the total in cell C3. Remember to use parenthesis to surround the part of the formula you wish Excel to do first: the adding of B6 and B7. The formula should look like this =(B6+B7)*C3 and the total should be 378.

	X Microsoft Excel - Book1										
	File Edit View Insert Format Tools Data Window Help										
	Courier New 10 B I U $ % ,										
	D6	=	=(B6+B7)*C3								
	A	B	C	D	E	F	G	H	I	J	
1			6								
2			7								
3			42								
4											
5		Testing									
6		4		378							
7		5									
8		9									
9											

To use the automatic SUM formula, you would start with the equal sign (=), followed by the word SUM and then a left parenthesis. Inside the parenthesis you would put the cell address of the first cell, followed by a colon, and then the cell address of the last cell. Now type a right parenthesis. In cell D1 type =SUM(B6:B7) and you will get a total of 9. You are now ready to begin.

On additional note, although the latest version of Excel – Excel 2007 – has some cosmetic updates, the fundamental functions and features remain basically the same. Besides, in the light of the fact that the existing versions of Excel (2003, 2000 and 97) are still in wide use, we will continue to use the existing versions for our examples. The following figures are introduced just for your reference and illustrate the cosmetic changes in Excel 2007.

To fully utilize the features that we will use throughout this book also in Excel 2007, you will need to activate some options as follows.

Locate the "Add-Ins" tab from the "Excel Options" box and click on "Go" button at the bottom with "Excel Add-Ins" selected in the "Manage" window.

Check "Analysis ToolPack" and "Solver Add-in" options for later uses in this book.

Chapter 4 Problems

Reconciliation statements are one type of item a spreadsheet handles well. You can enter outstanding check amounts, deposits not credited, bank fees and charges and have Excel complete the reconciliation. The file can be a template that can be used over and over again. We will be using problem 4-7 and create a reconciliation statement for Ben Luna's account.

We will need two areas: 1) Checkbook Balance and 2) Bank Balance. We will use abbreviations and change the number format to currency. Formulas will be entered where needed. NOTE: <u>ALL FORMULAS APPEAR IN APPENDIX A IN CASE YOU HAVE ANY DIFFICULTY</u>.

To be sure we have enough room in each cell we will first widen the cells and change the cells to a currency format. In the upper left hand corner, to the left of the letter A and directly above the number 1, there is a blank box. When you click on that box it will change the entire spreadsheet. Click on it now and the spreadsheet will highlight in grayish blue. Now click on the "$" symbol in the format task bar. Next click on the FORMAT menu; select COLUMNS; select WITH; and then type in the number 12. All the cells are set for currency and all the cells are set for a width of 12 characters.

Now click on cell A1. In cell A1 type the word "Checkbook". Next in cell A3 type the word "Balance:". In cell A4 type the word "Interest:". In cell A7 type the words "NSF:". In A8 type in "Mortgage:". In cell A9 type the word "Teller fee:". In A10 type in "Printing fee:". In cell A11 type the words "ATM fee:". And in cell A13 type the word: "Total:".

In cell D1 type the words "Bank Statement". In cell D3 type "Balance:". In cell D5 type "Deposit in Transit". In cell D6 type the words "Outstanding Checks:" for checks not yet deducted. In D7 and D8 type in #234 and #235 each. In cell D13 type the word "Total". Now we are ready to put the figures and formulas into place.

1) In B3 enter 1,1395.18.
2) In B4 enter 1.23.
3) In B7 enter –11.25.
4) In B8 enter –817.75
2) In B9 enter –3.
3) In B10 enter –3.5.
4) In B11 enter –6.4.
5) Now in B14 we enter "=sum(b3:b11)" and hit enter key. Alternatively, you may also just highlight the relevant data range into the parenthesis of the formula. The colon ":" means "through" indicating the range of data from the starting point to the ending point. Don't bother with upper or lower case characters. Once you hit the enter key, all the formula will automatically turn into upper case. (See Appendix A if you have trouble with the formula.)
6) Highlight and select the cells b3 through b11 and locate the "$"sign icon from the tool bar and click it. All the figures will automatically turn into currency, and all the negative values will be either in parenthesis, in red font, or preceded by minus sign depending on your computer's default setting.
7) In E3 enter 119.17.
8) In E4 enter 530.50.
9) In E7 enter –80.30.
10) In E8 enter –28.55.
11) In E 13 enter "=sum(e3:e11)". Alternatively, you may highlight the cell range to be added only up to E8 where data exist. However, it would be convenient to coincide the data range with the longer side in case there have been more transactions in the shorter side.

Alternatively, you can perform the same task using minus signs as follows.

RATE	▼	✕ ✓ =	=SUM(B3:B11)				

	A	B	C	D	E	F	G
1	**Checkbook**			**Bank Statement**			
2							
3	Balance:	$ 1,395.28		Balance:	$ 119.17		
4	Interest:	$ 1.23		Deposit in Transit:	$ 530.50		
5						Doc J:	
6				Outstanding Checks:		Using a minus sign wherever applicable, one can simply sum everything in the column.	
7	NSF:	($27.04)		# 234	$ (80.30)		
8	Mortgage	$ (815.75)		# 235	$ (28.55)		
9	Teller fee:	$ (3.00)					
10	Printing fee:	$ (3.50)				Doc J:	
11	ATM fee:	$ (6.40)				Using a minus sign wherever applicable, one can simply sum everything in the column.	
12							
13	Total:	=SUM(B3:B11)		Total:	$ 540.82		
14							
15							
16							

Before proceeding, you should save this file to your disk. This is a template you can use over and over. Click on FILE and click on SAVE AS. Enter the filename "C4" for Chapter 4. Be sure the file is set for your disk. Ask the lab assistant for help.

You can now erase the figures and enter new figures. Be careful NOT to erase the formulas.

PROBLEM: Using this reconciliation template, take your own checkbook or a checkbook from a business or company and see if you can make the balances match.

Chapter 6 Problems

Spreadsheets do not have to be elaborate to do the job. The WORD PROBLEMS 6-52 and 6-53 ask for two different numbers but they refer to the same base (the base will be the denominator in the percent problem). You can set up a spreadsheet to do both problems at once.

We must change column C to percentages. First click on the letter C above the C column. The entire column will turn dark except for cell C1. Then click on the FORMAT menu; click on the CELLS command; click on the word PERCENTAGE on the LEFT side of the information box and then click on the OK button. Now the column is set for percentages.

Use A1 for our heading and type "Dunkin Donut's Survey" (again the overflow is automatic).

Go to cell A3 and type "Base".

Go to cell A5 and type "Coffee".

Go to cell A7 and type "No Coffee".

Go to B7. The formula will calculate the number of non-diet drinkers by subtracting the number of diet drinkers in cell B5 from the base in cell B3. (See Appendix A).

Go to C5. The formula will take the number of diet drinkers from B5 and divide them by the base number of B3 (disregard the results for now). (See Appendix A).

Go to C7. The formula must take the number of non-diet drinkers from B7 and divide them by the base number of B3 (disregard the results for now). (See Appendix A). Save the template to your disk if you wish.

The template will look like this:

	A	B	C
1	Dunkin Donut's Survey		
2			
3	Base:		
4			
5	Coffee:		=B5/$B$7
6			
7	No Coffee:	=B3-B5	=B7/$B$7
8			
9			
10			

In cell B3 enter the base number of 12,000.

In cell B5 enter the diet drinkers number 3,000.

The formulas will automatically calculate.

PROBLEM: Build a template to find the answer to this question: The Gallup Poll interviews 850 people about their choice of candidate. 375 people prefer Senator Halley while the rest prefer Senator Johnson. What percentages does each Senator have?

Chapter 7 Problems

Spreadsheets can help compare different values. In this case we will be using the SUMMARY PRACTICE TEST problem number 7 to help Pat Mann decide whether manufacturer A or manufacturer B is offering her the best value.

First we change the format of the values. Take the cell pointer and place it on the rectangle just ABOVE the row numbers and to the LEFT of the column letters and click. The entire spreadsheet has turned dark except for cell A1. Now click on the TASKBAR button that looks like a comma (,) to set for numbers.

In cell A1 type "Man. A".

In cell D1 type "Man. B".

In cell A2 type "First". Do the same in cell D2.

In cell B2 type "Second". Do the same in cell E2.

In cell A7 type "Discount". Do the same in cell D7.

In cell A5 enter the formula that will take 1.00 and subtract the value in A3 (disregard the answer for now). (See Appendix A).

In cell B5 enter the formula that will take 1.00 and subtract the value of B3 (disregard the answer for now). (See Appendix A).

In cell B7 enter the formula that will take the answer from A5, multiply it times the answer in B5, and subtract that from 1.000 (disregard the answer for now). (See Appendix A).

In cell D5 enter the formula that will take 1.00 and subtract the value of D3 (disregard the answer for now). (See Appendix A).

In cell E5 enter the formula that will take 1.00 and subtract the value of E3 (disregard the answer for now). (See Appendix A).

In cell E7 enter the formula that will take the answer from D5, multiply it times the answer in E5, and subtract that from 1.000 (disregard the answer for now). (See Appendix A). Save if you wish.

Your spreadsheet should look like this:

	A	B	C	D	E	F
1	Man. A			Man. B		
2	First	Second		First	Second	
3						
4						
5	1	1		1	1	
6						
7	Discount	0			0	
8						

We are now ready to enter the information.

Go to cell A3 and enter ".14".

Go to cell B3 and enter ".08".

Go to cell D3 and enter ".15".

Go to cell E3 and enter ".07".

All the formulas will calculate and you can now compare the discount for Manufacturer A in cell B7 with discount for Manufacturer B in cell E7. You will find that Manufacturer A gives the best discount.

PROBLEM: You are ordering new computers from COMPWORLD. They offer you a choice of discount plans. Plan A offers you 14/10 and Plan B offers you 25/4. Which of the plans is best for you?

Chapter 8 Problems

In this chapter we will be calculating a final price that has gone through a number of markdowns and markups. We will show the price through each change as well as the final selling price and the markdown percent. We will use the information in PROBLEM 8-15.

First we change the way the values will appear. Go to the row number 3 and click on it. The entire row turns black except for cell A3. Next click on the CURRENCY button ($) in the TASKBAR. Click cell F3 and click on the PERCENT button (%) in the TASKBAR and INCREASE the number of decimals by 2.

In cell A1 type "Original". In cell A2 type "Selling Price".

In cell B1 type "First". In cell B2 type "Markdown".

In cell C1 type "Second". In cell C2 type "Markdown".

In cell E1 type "Final". In cell E2 type "Markdown".

In cell F1 type "Markdown". In cell F2 type "Percentage".

In cell D2 type "Markup".

You should now adjust your columns by using the FORMAT menu and COLUMN choice as you did before. Your spreadsheet should look like this:

	A	B	C	D	E	F	G
1	Original	First	Second		Final	Markdown	
2	Selling Price	Markdown	Markdown	Markup	Markdown	Percentage	
3		$ -	$ -	$ -	$ -	#DIV/0!	
4							

In cell A3 enter the figure $5,000.

Enter the formulas keeping in mind you must subtract or add the percentages given from 100% depending on if it is a markdown or a markup. In cell B3 enter the formula that will take the value of B3 (it is a markdown), and multiply by A3.

In cell C3 enter the formula that will take the value of C3, (it is a markdown), and multiply by B3.

In cell D3 enter the formula that will take the value of D3, (it is a markup), and multiply by C3.

In cell E3 enter the formula that will take the value of E3, (it is a markdown), and multiply by D3.

As the formulas should calculate and you will find the totals will be:

$4,000 for first markdown; $3,600 for second markdown; $4,032 for the markup; $3830.40 for the final markdown; and 23.39% for final percentage.

PROBLEM: Your boss put you in charge of changing the price each time a new markdown is taken. You need to keep track of each price change and what the final percentage will be. The original selling price is $300.00.

Markdowns: First is 5%, Second is 12%, Markup is 3%, and the Final is 18%.

Breakeven Analysis

We will use **summary practice test** #11 for example. There are largely two ways to perform breakeven analysis using Excel. The first one is by building the format and entering relevant data and formula to solve for the breakeven output level (Q_{BE}), and the second one is by using Excel's built-in **"Goal Seek"** function.

We will look into the formula method first. We build the table as in the following figure. Ignore columns D and E for now. We build just one table across columns A and B only.

In cell A1, type "Parameters", which are the given data.
In cell A2, type "P" for selling price, and enter 25.99 in cell B2.
Highlight column B and select $ sign from the tool bar, so that the entire column will be formatted as currency.
In cell A3, type "TFC" for Total fixed cost, and enter 80960 in cell B3
In cell A4, type "AVC" for Average variable cost, or the unit cost, and enter 18.95 in B4.
In cell A6, type "Variables", which are the unknowns to solve for. In our problem, this is the output level (quantity) at breakeven. Enter the formula for break even B6 as shown in the figure below.
In cell A9, type "Results".
In cell A10, type "TR" for Total revenue, and enter the formula in cell B10 as in the figure.
In cell A11, type "TFC", and simply enter B3 to point to the cell that already contains the data.
In cell A12, type "TVC" for Total variable cost, and enter the formula in cell B12 as in the figure.
In cell A13, type "TC" for Total cost which is TFC+TVC, and enter the formula in cell B13 as in the figure.
In cell A14, type profit, which is TR-TC, and enter the formula in cell B14 as in the figure.
Since profit=$0 by definition at breakeven point, once Q_{BE} in cell B7 is solved for, cell B14 will automatically show $ - for 0.

	A	B	C	D	E	F
1	Parameters			Parameters		
2	P	25.99		P	25.99	
3	TFC	80960		TFC	80960	
4	AVC	18.95		AVC	18.95	
5						
6	Variables			Variables		
7	Q	=B3/(B2−B4)		Q	11500	Doc J: This cell is the goal to solve for, and hence, should not already contain any formula in it.
8				By Goal Seek		
9	Results			Results		
10	TR	=B2*B7		TR	=E2*E7	
11	TFC	=B3		TFC	=E3	
12	TVC	=B4*B7		TVC	=E4*E7	
13	TC	=B11+B12		TC	=E11+E12	
14	Profit	=B10−B13		Profit	=E10−E13	
15						

Now, we will use "Goal Seek" to perform breakeven analysis. We can copy the existing format for this purpose. Simply highlight the entire format and copy it into cell D1. Although you just select one single cell, Excel will automatically paste the whole table over into the correct range of cells.

The only difference between the previous method and this one is that the solution formula is not assumed – *i.e.* we leave the cell D7 blank, and let Excel worry about it. In order for Excel to find the solution, click on "Tools" menu in the tool bar on top. Once the drop-down menu opens up, select "Goal Seek", and the Goal Seek dialogue box will open up.

Click on the spreadsheet icon in the right corner to enter the target cell into the "Set cell:" box. This is the goal (profit) we want to set to $0. Why? Because by definition, profit=$0 at breakeven. So, we enter "0" in the next box to set it to value of "0". Then, click on the spreadsheet icon in the right corner of "By changing cell:" box to enter cell E7, the unknown we want to solve for. Intuitively, this is the cell that is supposed to contain the data we must vary to arrive at the $0 profit we have set for breakeven point.

C	D	E	F	G	H	I
	Parameters					
	P	$ 25.99	**Doc J:** This cell is the goal to solve for,			
	TFC	$ 80,960.00	and hence, should not already			
	AVC	$ 18.95	contain any formula in it.			
	Variables					
	Q					
	Results		**Goal Seek**			
	TR	$ –	Set cell:	$E$14		
	TFC	$ 80,960.00	To value:	0		
	TVC	$ –	By changing cell:	$E$7		
	TC	$ 80,960.00	OK	Cancel		
	Profit	$ (80,960.00)				

Then, we click O.K., and the result will be instantly calculated as follows.

D	E	F	G	H	I
Parameters					
P	$ 25.99	**Doc J:** This cell is the goal to solve for,			
TFC	$ 80,960.00	and hence, should not already			
AVC	$ 18.95	contain any formula in it.			
Variables					
Q	$ 11,500.00	**Goal Seek Status**			
		Goal Seeking with Cell E14 found a solution.	OK		
Results			Cancel		
TR	$ 298,885.00	Target value: 0	Step		
TFC	$ 80,960.00	Current value: $-			
TVC	$ 217,925.00		Pause		
TC	$ 298,885.00				
Profit	$ –				

Chapter 9 Problems

Computing payrolls is made easier with spreadsheets using formulas which automatically change when you change the salary. Here we will be doing the PROBLEMS 9-12 and 13, setting up a payroll spreadsheet for Ring and Porter so they can compute their total earnings. They can use the same spreadsheet each week to compute their earnings by entering the new numbers.

In cell A2 type "Gross Sales:".

In cell A4 type "Return:".

In cell A6 type "Net Sales:".

In cell A8 type "Given Quota:".

In cell A10 type "Commission Sales:".

In cell A12 type "Commission Rates:".

In cell A14 type "Total Commission:".

In cell A16 type "Regular Wage:".

In cell A18 type "Total Wage:"

Your spreadsheet should look like this:

	A	B	C	D
1		Ring	Porter	
2	Gross Sales:			
3				
4	Return:			
5				
6	Net Sales:	=B2-B4	=C2-C4	
7				
8	Given Quota:			
9				
10	Commission Sales:	=B6-B8	=C6-C8	
11				
12	Commission Rates:			
13				
14	Total Commission:	=B10*B12	=C10*C12	
15				
16	Regular Wage:			
17				
18	Total Wage:	=B14+B16	=C14+C16	
19				

Now we can enter the dollar amounts, commission rate and formulas to calculate the salary.

In cells B1 and C1 enter the employees' names, Ring and Porter respectively.

In cell B2 and C2 enter the gross sales. Then click on the currency symbol "$" in the task bar to make the figure into currency.

In cell B4 and C4 enter the amount of returns.

In cell B6 and C6 enter the formula that will calculate the net sales. Then click on the currency symbol "$" in the task bar to make the figure into currency.

In cell B8 and C8 enter the given quota. Then click on the currency symbol "$" in the task bar to make the figure into currency.

In cell B10 and C10 enter the commission sales, and click on the currency symbol "$".

In cell B12 and C12 enter the commission rate in decimal format. You may also click on % icon in the tool bar to make these figures into percentage.

In cell B14 and C14 enter the formula to calculate the total sales commission. Then click on the currency symbol "$" in the task bar to make the figure into currency.

In cell B16 and C16 enter the regular wage, and click on the currency symbol "$".

Now you are ready for the final step. In cell B18 and C18 enter the formula that will add the regular wage to the total commission. Then click on the currency symbol "$" in the task bar to make the figure into currency.

PROBLEM: John Franks works for $8.75 per hour and worked a 40 hour week. He also gets commission on sales. His sales were $2,650 and his commission rate is 4%. Calculate his total pay.

Chapter 10 Problems

We will set up a table to calculate maturity value using ordinary interest, the method used by most banks. This spreadsheet will be used for Problems 10-4, 10-5, and 10-6 in your text. The formula to use is:

$$T = \frac{\text{Exact Number of Days}}{360}$$

We will set three columns to currency and also widen them. By holding down the CONTROL key (marked CTRL) you can select all three columns and all three will stay active. Hold down the CONTROL key and click on the column letters A, F, G. Click CURRENCY symbol ($). Immediately click on the FORMAT menu; click on the COLUMN command; click on the WIDTH choice and a box will open for the desired width. Type "15". Now click on the OK button and all three columns are now set for currency and are now 15 picas wide.

In cell A1 type "Principal".

In cell B1 type "Interest Rate".

In cell C1 type "Date Borrowed".

In cell D1 type "Date Repaid".

In cell E1 type "Time".

In cell F1 type "Interest".

In cell G1 type "Future (Maturity) Value".

(Remember: If the labels are too long, click on "Format" in the tool bar, select "Cells", click on "Alignment" tab, and check the box for "Wrap text".)

In cell E2 enter the formula to calculate the time which is the repaid date in D2 minus the borrowed date in C2. (Dates can be formatted as mm/dd/yyyy.)

In cell F2 enter the formula to calculate the interest by using the principal from A2 times the rate in B2 (Enter decimal and click on % sign on the toolbar.) times the calculation for T (T = the exact number of days in E2 divided by 360).

Lastly in cell G2 enter the formula to calculate the Maturity Value by adding the principal in A2 to the interest in F2.

Your spreadsheet should look like this:

	A	B	C	D	E	F	G	H
1	Principal	Interest Rate	Date Borrowed	Date Repaid	Exact Time	Interest	Future (Maturity) Value	
2					0.00	$ –	$ –	
3					0.00	$ –	$ –	
4					0.00	$ –	$ –	
5								

Enter the data from the problems beginning with problem 10-4.

In cell A2 enter the principal of $1,000.

In cell B2 enter the decimal of 8%.

In cell C2 enter the number for the date corresponding to March 8 which you will find in your Business Math Handbook. (You did this in Chapter 7.)

In cell D2 enter the number for the date corresponding to June 9. Again you will find it in your Business Math Handbook.

You should arrive at the answer of 93 days for time; $20.67 for interest; and $1,020.67 for maturity value. You can now enter the other values in rows A3 and A4 along with the proper formulas.

PROBLEM: Change the template to calculate the EXACT interest method used by the Federal Reserve (365 days). You will have to change the formula in cell F2 (see Appendix A). Use the following data: $2500 principal, 7% interest rate, borrowed on April 11, and repaid on August 18.

Chapter 11 Problems

This chapter's problem involves finding the amount of interest charged for each note, the amount the borrower would receive, the amount the payee would receive at maturity and the effective rate. We will use the figures from Summary Practice Test 2 in the text. The spreadsheet will use only two columns: 1) column A will be for titles, and 2) column B will be for formulas and data.

In cell A1 type "Face Value:".

In cell A2 type "Discount Percent:".

In cell A3 type "Number of Days:".

In cell A4 type "Interest Charged:".

In cell A5 type "Borrower Received".

In cell A6 type "Amount at Maturity".

In cell A7 type "Effective Rate".

Adjust the cell width for both the titles and the formulas. Click on the rectangle above the row numbers and to the left of the column letters; click on FORMAT menu; click on the COLUMN command; click on STANDARD WIDTH and type in the number 20; click on the OK button. You will only see four columns on the screen now. Your spreadsheet will look like this:

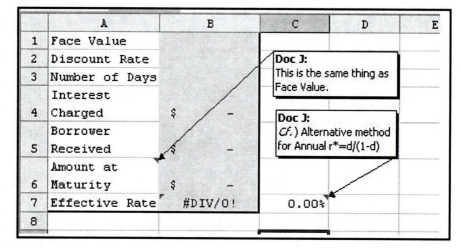

Finally, adjust the value format of cells B1, B4, B5, and B6 to CURRENCY format. Holding the CONTROL key (CTRL) click on cells B1, B4, B5, and B6. Click on the CURRENCY button ($).

Adjust cells B2 and B7 to PERCENTAGES by clicking on cell B2 and hold the CONTROL key and click on cell B7. Click on the PERCENTAGE button (%). You will need to increase the decimals by one using the INCREASE DECIMAL button on the keyboard. Click once.

Now we enter the figures and formulas. Remember, if you have any difficulty with formulas you should go to Appendix A.

In cell B1 you enter the face value figure.

In cell B2 you enter the discount percent figure.

In cell B3 you enter the number of days.

In cell B4 you enter the formula to calculate interest charged.

In cell B5 you enter the formula to calculate amount borrower received.

In cell B6 you enter the formula to calculate amount at maturity.

In cell B7 you enter the formula to calculate the effective rate rounding off to the nearest tenth percent.

The formulas will automatically calculate as you enter this data. You will find the interest rate charged is $302.22; the amount the borrower would receive is $16,697.78; and the effective rate will be 4.1%.

PROBLEM: You go to a bank and get a simple discount note for $6,500. The interest rate is 6% for 100 days. Calculate the interest charged, the amount you receive, the amount the payee would receive at maturity, and the effective rate.

Chapter 12 Problems

We will be calculating present value for problems 12-7, 12-8, 12-9, and 12-10

Three columns need to have the value format and the width changed. In addition you will need to use the **PV Table 12-3** from the textbook.

Hold the CONTROL key down and click on the column letters A, D, and H. Click on the CURRENCY button ($). Immediately click on the FORMAT menu, click on COLUMN command, click on WIDTH choice, type in the number 12, and click on the OK button. Now click on cell F2 and decrease the number of decimals by clicking once on the DECREASE DECIMAL button.

In cell A1 type "Target Amount".

In cell B1 type "Time (in Years)".

In cell C1 type "APR (Set Rate)".

In cell D1 type "Compounding Frequency".

In cell E1 type "Time (Periods)".

In cell F1 type "Periodic Rate".

In cell G1 type "Factor".

In cell H1 type "PV Amount".

We can now enter our formulas. If you have any problems with a formula see appendix A.

In cell E2 type the formula for the period used. Take the years in cell B2 and multiply by 2 (semiannual).

In cell F2 type the formula for the rate used. Take the rate in cell C2 and divide by 2 (semiannual).

In cell H2 type the formula to give you the PV of amount desired at the end of the period. Take the amount in A2 and multiply it by the PV factor you entered from the table in cell G2.

The spreadsheet should look like this:

	A2	▼	=					
	A	**B**	**C**	**D**	**E**	**F**	**G**	**H**
1	Target Amount	Time (in Years)	APR (Set Rate)	Compounding Frequency	Time (Periods)	Periodic Rate	Factor	PV
2								
3								

Now enter the data from **Problem 12-7**.

In cell A2 enter the amount desired at the end of period.

In cell B2 enter the length of time.

In cell C2 enter the rate.

In cell D2 type "semiannual".

The PV period used and rate used have automatically appeared. Using those figures, go to **PV Table 12-3** in your book and type in the PV factor. (That factor should be .7885.)

The final column for PV amount desired at end of period will automatically calculate and should be $2,050.10.

You can now do problems 12-8, 12-9, and 12-10. **Remember that you must adjust the formulas in cells E2 and F2 to reflect the new compounded time frame**. See Appendix A if you have difficulty changing the formulas.

An alternative approach would be as follows. This approach will allow you to calculate it solely with Excel without relying on the PVIF table. This technique has many advantages over the use of the table, because there are no restrictions in the length or chunk of timeframe or the number of decimal places in the rate as in the table.

We build the table in a similar manner as in the previous method. However, this time we will directly enter the formula for **PV** in our solution cell.

$$PV = \frac{FV}{\left(1 + \dfrac{r}{f}\right)^{nf}} \text{, where}$$

FV = Future Value or Amount at Maturity

r = stated rate or set rate

f = compound frequency per year

n = number of years to maturity

Now, the spreadsheet would look like this.

B2		▼	=			
	A	B	C	D	E	F
1		Target Amount	t (in yrs)	APR	frequency	PV
2	P12-7					=B2/(1+D2/E2)^(C2*E2)
3	P12-8					=B3/(1+D3/E3)^(C3*E3)
4	P12-9					=B4/(1+D4/E4)^(C4*E4)
5	P12-10					=B5/(1+D5/E5)^(C5*E5)
6						
7						

In cell B2 enter the amount desired at the end of period.
In cell C2 enter the length of time in years. If it is not in discrete number of years, such as 2 years and 3 months, we need to convert it into fraction of years such as 2.25 years. (3 months = ¼ year = 0.25 year)

In cell D2 enter the stated rate or set rate.

In cell E2 enter the compounding frequency per year. For example, if it is annual – *i.e.* interest is compounded only once at the end of the year, enter 1; if semiannual (compounded every 6 months), enter 2; if quarterly (every 3 months), enter 4; if monthly, enter 12. We need to adjust the stated annual rate to an appropriate rate for each compounding period by dividing the stated rate by this frequency, because the state rate of 4%, for example, certainly won't accrue every quarter, but rather by 1% per quarter.

In cell F2, enter the above formula for **PV**. In our problem 12-7, it should be entered as "=b2(1+d2/e2)^c2*e2", where "^" symbol represents **raised to power of...**". Once you have solved 12-7, the rest of the problems can be solved automatically by copying and pasting the formula into cells F3 through F5 if the given data are already filled in for the rest of the problems.

PROBLEM: The amount desired is $3,000 held for 5 years at a rate of 6%. What is the PV mount if the rate is compounded monthly? Quarterly? Annually?

Chapter 13 Problems

Problem 13-23 places Joe Martin in a difficult situation. His uncle will give him cash or money in an annuity. Joe's problem is to decide which is better.

First we change the cell widths by clicking on the SELECT ENTIRE SPREADSHEET box with is the small rectangle to the LEFT of the column A letter and above the row 1 number. Now click on the FORMAT menu; click on the COLUMN command; click on WIDTH choice; type the number "12".

Now hold the CONTROL key (CTRL) and click on cells A3 and E2 and click the CURRENCY button ($). Lastly hold the CONTROL key (CTRL) and click cells A5 and C2 and click the PERCENTAGE button (%).

In cell A1 type "Quarter", in A2 type "Amount", in cell A4 type "Interest" and in cell A6 type "Years".

In cell C1 type "Rate", in cell C3 type "Periods", in cell D1 type "Table 13-2" and in cell E1 type "Annuity".

Now you are ready to enter the formulas you will need. If you have any problems with the formulas see appendix A.

In cell C2 enter the formula to compute the interest rate. This is the interest in A5 divided by four.

In cell C4 enter the formula to compute the number of periods. This is the years in A7 times four.

In cell E2 enter the formula for the annuity. This would be the table rate in cell D2 times the quarter amount in A3. The spreadsheet looks like this:

	A	B	C	D	E
1	Quarter		Rate	TABLE 13-2	Annuity
2	Amount		#DIV/0!		$ -
3			Periods		
4	Interest		#DIV/0!		
5					
6	Years				
7					

We enter the data from the text.

In cell A3 enter the amount of the gift ($900).

In cell A5 enter the percentage.

In cell A7 enter the number of years.

In cell D2 enter the table value from Table 13-2.

When you compare the annuity amount in cell E2 with the cash gift of $12,000 the choice is obvious. Joe should take the annuity.

As is the case with Chapter 12, an alternative approach is to enter the Present Value of Annuity (**PVA**) formula directly into the solution cell. Once again, the benefit of this approach is the freedom from dependency on the table that is bound to limitations in terms of timeframe and precision in the range of rates… etc. Also, the accuracy in the values we solve for is an added advantage of this technique.

The **PVA** can be defined as follows:

$$PVA = \frac{PMT}{r} - \frac{PMT}{r(1+r)^n}, \text{ where}$$

PMT = regular annuity payment

r = stated annual rate adjusted for the frequency of payment per year

n = number of payments

or $PVA = -\dfrac{PMT}{r}\left[\dfrac{1}{(1+r)^n}-1\right]$ if we factor out $-\dfrac{1}{r}\left[\dfrac{1}{(1+r)^n}-1\right]$, which is exactly how the **PVAIF**

(Present Value of Annuity Interest Factor)is calculated in the table.

Now, we build the following table, where

	A	B	C	D	E	F	G
1	PMT	int	f	r	t	n	PVA
2				=B2/C2		=C2*E2	=A2/D2-A2/(D2*(1+D2)^F2)
3							
4							

int = stated APR or set rate

f = compound or payment frequency per year

r = stated annual rate adjusted for the frequency of payment per year $\left(r = \dfrac{int}{f}\right)$

t = number of years to maturity

n = number of payments to maturity $\left(n = f \times t\right)$

Now, enter the data and you will instantly have the result exactly to the cent as follows.

	A	B	C	D	E	F	G	H
1	PMT	int	f	r	t	n	PVA	
2	$900.00	8%	4	2%	4	16	$ 12,219.94	
3								
4								

PROBLEM: Your Great Aunt Pheobe sends a gift on the birth of your first child. She is offering $10,000 or a quarterly annuity of $1,000 for three years. At 8% interest for the annuity, which would you take?

Chapter 14 Problems

When purchasing an automobile, most of us will pay over time. This spreadsheet will find the finance charge, deferred payment, monthly payment, and the APR. We will use Problem 14-10 from the text to finance the home improvement project and Problem 14-15 to finance Toyota hybrid.

First we widen all the columns. Click on the FORMAT menu; click on the COLUMN command; click on STANDARD WIDTH; type the number 16; click on the OK button.

Now set the currency format. Hold the CONTROL key (CTRL) down and click on B1, B2, B4, D1 and D2 being careful not to let go of the CONTROL key. After clicking on all cells let go of the CONTROL key. Click on the CURRENCY button ($).

In cell A1 type "Project Amount".

In cell A2 type "Number of Months".

In cell A3 type "Down Pay @".

In cell A4 type "Payment Frequency".

In cell A5 type "Loss to credit limit cut (Finance Charge)".

In cell D1 type "Loan Amount".

In cell D2 type "Down Payment".

In cell D3 type "Interest Rate".

In cell D4 type "Periodic Rate".

In cell D5 type "Monthly Payment".

Your spreadsheet should look like this:

	B5	▼	=		
	A	B	C	D	E
1	Project Amount			Loan Amount	
2	Number of Months			Down Payment	
3	Downpay @			Interest Rate	
4	Payment Frequency			Periodic Rate	
5	Loss to credit limit cut (Finance Charge)			Monthly Payment	

We will now enter the data from your text.

In cell B1 enter $8.500.

In cell B2 enter 12.

In cell B3 enter 10%.

In cell B4 enter 12.

In cell B5 enter the formula for finance charge.

In cell E1 enter the formula for the amount financed.

In cell E2 enter the formula for down payment.

In cell E3 enter 11%.

In cell E4 enter the formula for periodic rate.

In cell E5 enter the formula for monthly payment.

Another application of this type of problem is a model to find the regular (monthly) payment amount. While the above problem is mainly addressing the issue of finance charges (total amount of interest), which is a fairly simple and straight-forward task with everything already known, people are usually also keen to know if their monthly payment is an accurately calculated, fair and legitimate amount. It is called amortization problem, because it is usually the method used to amortize or pay down debt.

Although the above example also addresses the monthly payment, but the method relies heavily on the look-up factor table (**PVAIF**), which is rather crude and cumbersome, since the calculation is bound to be severely restricted by the range of the table and the precise degree of decimal places used in the table. Besides, the table is not something ubiquitously available. It cannot be conveniently carried around on you any time any where. These are certainly just a few of the many shortcomings of the table method.

For example, if you finance your car, you owe the finance company the dealership price of the car plus the finance charges, which is equivalent to the purchase price in the above format. So over the next X-number of months (periods), you amortize or pay down this amount in X-number of equal payments. Although this monthly payment amount is always the same, the way it is structured – *i.e.* the ratio by which it is split between principal owed (debt or the dealership price) and finance charges (interest) - changes over time. It is usually structured in such a way that the most interest is to be paid early on and to decrease as time goes by, whereas the least principal is to be paid early on and to increase as the number of payments advances.

Viewed from the finance company's perspective, this is exactly the annuity, because they are receiving a stream of even payments periodically until the full maturity value is paid up. So, this is exactly the flip side of the same coin, and the solution is the reverse process of the **PVA** problem. In other words, in a **PVA** problem, our objective is to solve for the **PVA,** given other variables. In an amortization problem, the objective is to solve it for the **PMT,** given other variables.

We know that the **PVA** can be found by the following formula:

$$PVA = \frac{PMT}{r} - \frac{PMT}{r(1+r)^n} \text{, where}$$

PMT = regular annuity payment

r = stated annual rate adjusted for the frequency of payment per year

n = number of payments

$$\text{or } PVA = -\frac{PMT}{r}\left[\frac{1}{(1+r)^n} - 1\right]$$

And since it is the **PMT** this time that we want to find out while everything else is known, all we need to do is solve this equation for **PMT**:

$$PMT = PVA\left[\frac{r(1+r)^n}{(1+r)^n-1}\right]$$

So, we can now apply this formula to Problem 14-10 assuming that all else is given to solve for the monthly payment. If this figure is equal to the value already given in the problem, our solution checks out.

Now the solution can be programmed as follows.

B5		=	=E5*B2-E1		
	A	B	C	D	E
1	Project Amount	8500		Loan Amount	=B1-E2
2	Number of Months	12		Down Payment	=B1*B3
3	Downpay @	0.1		Interest Rate	0.11
4	Payment Frequency	12		Periodic Rate	=E3/B4
5	Loss to credit limit cut (Finance Charge)	=E5*B2-E1		Monthly Payment	=E1*(E4*(1+E4)^B2)/((1+E4)^B2-1)
6					
7					

Once the given data are entered, then the solution is obtained instantly.

B5		=	=E5*B2-E1			
	A	B	C	D	E	F
1	Project Amount	$8,500.00		Loan Amount	$7,650.00	
2	Number of Months	12.00		Down Payment	$ 850.00	
3	Downpay @	10%		Interest Rate	11.00%	
4	Payment Frequency	12.00		Periodic Rate	0.92%	
5	Loss to credit limit cut (Finance Charge)	$ 463.44		Monthly Payment	$ 676.12	
6						
7						

Our computed solution is a little different from the solution obtained from the table. This is mainly the rounding error, but the computed solution is undoubtedly the most accurate, because the value from the **PVAIF** look-up table itself wasn't the exact value to begin with. (Remember that sometimes the values in the table are at best approximations, not exact to the dot, so we are forced to take the value that is the nearer of the two adjacent values in the table. - *Cf.* LU 14-1) That is why there's a clear benefit in programming the formula into the model.

We may also formulate it alternatively as follows.

	A	B	C	D	E	F	G
1	PVA (Loan)	int (APR)	PMT freq	periodic r	t (in yr)	n (=f*t)	PMT
2	=E15	=E17	12	=B2/C2	1	=C2*E2	=(A2*(D2*(1+D2)^F2)
3							

	A	B	C PMT freq	D	E	F	G
1	PVA (Loan)	int (APR)		periodic r	t (in yr)	n (=f*t)	PMT
2	$7,650.00	11.00%	12	0.92%	1	12	$ 676.12

Now, let's build a model to solve 14-15 as follows.

	A	B	C	D	E	F	G
1	a. Citizens Financial Bank						
2	Purchase Price	$ 18,999.00		Amount Financed	$ 16,999.00		
3	Number of Month:	48.00		Finance Charge	$ 2,920.77		
4	Down Payment	$ 2,000.00		Interest Rate	8.00%		
5	Trade-in	$ –		Periodic Rate	0.67%		
6	Frequency	12.00		Monthly Payment	$ 415.00		
7							
8	PVA (Loan)	int (APR)	PMT freq	periodic r	t (in yr)	n (=f*t)	PMT
9	$ 16,999.00	8.00%	12	0.67%	4	48	$415.00
10							
11	b. Charter One Bank						
12	Purchase Price	$ 18,999.00		Amount Financed	$ 16,999.00		
13	Number of Month:	60.00		Finance Charge	$ 3,438.51		
14	Down Payment	$ 2,000.00		Interest Rate	7.50%		
15	Trade-in	$ –		Periodic Rate	0.63%		
16	Frequency	12.00		Monthly Payment	$ 340.63		
17							
18	PVA (Loan)	int (APR)	PMT freq	periodic r	t (in yr)	n (=f*t)	PMT
19	$ 16,999.00	7.50%	12	0.63%	5	60	$340.63
20							
21	c. a-b =	$ 74.37					

PROBLEM: You see a Ford Thunderbird for sale with the following terms: Selling price of $28,500; $2,000 down; Financed for 48 months; with a monthly payment of $565.50. The APR is listed at 6.5%. Check to see if the dealership has the right figures for this car.

Chapter 15 Problems

Using a spreadsheet you can quickly calculate monthly payments for a home mortgage. We will be using the information from problems 15-1, 15-2, and 15-3 in your text.

The first step is to change to currency in columns A, B, C, F, and G. Hold the CONTROL key and click on the column letters A, B, C, F, and G making sure NOT to let go of the CONTROL key. Let go of the CONTROL key and click on the CURRENCY button ($).

In cell A1 type "Selling Price".

In cell B1 type "Money Down".

In cell C1 type "Principal".

In cell D1 type "Interest Rate".

In cell E1 type "Years".

In cell F1 type "Payment".

In cell G1 type "Per Month".

Now widen all the columns. Select the ENTIRE spreadsheet by clicking on the rectangle to the LEFT of the column A letter and above the row 1 number; click on the FORMAT menu; highlight the COLUMN command; click on the AUTOFIT SELECTION choice. Now click on the letter at the top of column C; click on the FORMAT menu; highlight the COLUMN command; click on WIDTH and enter the number 13.50 and click OK. Now we can enter the formulas. If you have any problems with the formulas, see appendix A.

In cell C2 enter the formula that will calculate the loan principal using the selling price minus the down payment.

In cell G2 enter the formula to calculate the monthly mortgage payment using the loan principal divided by 1000 and multiplying by the payment.

Your spreadsheet should look like this:

	A	B	C	D	E	F	G
1	Selling Price	Money Down	Principal	Interest Rate	Years	Payment	Per Month
2			$ -				$ -
3							

Enter the information in Problem 15-1 into the proper cells. In cell F2 enter the number from **TABLE 15-1** for the payment per $1,000.

Now you can substitute the values from problems 15-2 and 15-3.

This problem can also be done in the same manner as in Chapter 14 problems. We apply the same PMT formula.

$$PMT = PVA\left[\frac{r(1+r)^n}{(1+r)^n - 1}\right]$$

Build the table as follows.

	A	B	C	D	E	F	G	H	I	J
1		Sell Price	Downpay	Principal	int	f	Adjst r	Years	n	PMT
2	P15-1			=B2-C2			=E2/F2		=F2*H2	=(D2*(G2*(1+G2)^I2))/((1+G2)^I2-1)
3	P15-2			=B3-C3			=E3/F3		=F3*H3	=(D3*(G3*(1+G3)^I3))/((1+G3)^I3-1)
4	P15-3			=B4-C4			=E4/F4		=F4*H4	=(D4*(G4*(1+G4)^I4))/((1+G4)^I4-1)
5										
6										
7										

Once we enter formula in D2, G2, I2 and J2, we don't need to enter one for each problem. All we need to do is copy the desired cell and paste it over the desired range. We can automate it by first placing the mouse on the lower right-hand corner of the cell border, and then the thick white cross cursor will turn into a thin black cross. It means that Excel is ready to copy that cell. Hold the left mouse button and drag it down over the range of cells to paste it into. Once we fill the cells with the relevant values, the answers will instantly show up.

	A	B	C	D	E	F	G	H	I	J
1		Sell Price	Downpay	Principal	int	f	Adjst r	Years	n	PMT
2	P15-1	$ 140,000.00	$ 10,000.00	$ 130,000.00	7.00%	12.00	0.58%	25	300	$ 918.81
3	P15-2	$ 90,000.00	$ 5,000.00	$ 85,000.00	5.50%	12.00	0.46%	30	360	$ 482.62
4	P15-3	$ 340,000.00	$ 70,000.00	$ 270,000.00	6.00%	12.00	0.50%	35	420	$ 1,539.51
5										
6										

Again, there may be a slight difference from the values obtained from the PVAIF look-up table due to rounding. However, the numbers in the J column are the most accurate monthly payment figures, because they are calculated to the utmost degree of precision with no rounding.

PROBLEM: You plan on buying a house for $175,500 and you have $30,000 for a down payment. The loan is for 25 years at 6.75%. What is your monthly payment?

Chapter 16 Problems

In Chapter 16 we will complete problem 16-3: A horizontal analysis for the J. Brown Company.

In column A type each of the labels starting with "Assets" and ending with "Total liab. and owner's equity".

In cell B2 enter "Year 2012" and in cell C2 enter "Year 2011".

In cell D1 enter "Increase (Decrease)", in cell D2 "Amount" and in cell E2 enter "Percent.

Next adjust columns B, C, and D for currency. Click on B1. Hold the CONTROL key and click on the letters B, C, and D. Once the three columns are active let go of the CONTROL key and click on the CURRENCY button ($).

Now we change column E to percentages. Click on the letter E at the top of the E column and then click on the PERCENTAGE button (%).

Adjust the columns by clicking on the rectangle beside the column letter A and above the row number 1. Next click on the FORMAT menu; highlight the COLUMNS command; and then click on AUTOFIT SELECTION choice.

You will need the following formulas. If you have any problems with the formulas, see appendix A.

In cell B9 enter the formula to add the numbers from cash through prepaid advertising and copy formula to cell C9.

In cell B13 enter the formula to add total current assets to total plant and equipment and copy formula to cell C13.

In cell B18 enter the formula to add accounts payable and salaries payable and copy formula to cell C18.

In cell B22 enter the formula to add total current liabilities, long-term liabilities and J Brown capital (owner's equity) and copy formula to cell C22.

In column D enter the formulas to calculate the dollar amount of increase or decrease by using the 2012 amount minus the 2011 amount.

In column E enter the formulas that will calculate the percentage of change by using the dollar amount of the increase or decrease and dividing it by the 2011 amount.

Your spreadsheet will look like the following:

	A	B	C	D	E
1				Increase	(Decrease)
2		2012	2011	Amount	Percent
3	ASSETS				
4	Current Assets:			=B4-C4	=D4/C4
5	Cash			=B5-C5	=D5/C5
6	Accounts Receivable			=B6-C6	=D6/C6
7	Merchandise Inventory			=B7-C7	=D7/C7
8	Prepaid Advertising			=B8-C8	=D8/C8
9	Total Current Assets	=SUM(B5:B8)	=SUM(C5:C8)	=B9-C9	=D9/C9
10	Plant & Equipment			=B10-C10	=D10/C10
11	Building (net)			=B11-C11	=D11/C11
12	Land			=B12-C12	=D12/C12
13	Total Assets	=SUM(B9:B12)	=SUM(C9:C12)	=B13-C13	=D13/C13
14	LIABILITIES			=B14-C14	=D14/C14
15	Current Liabilites:			=B15-C15	=D15/C15
16	Accounts Payable			=B16-C16	=D16/C16
17	Salaries Payable			=B17-C17	=D17/C17
18	Total Current Liabilites	=SUM(B16:B17)	=SUM(C16:C17)	=B18-C18	=D18/C18
19	Long-term Liabilites			=B19-C19	=D19/C19
20	EQUITY			=B20-C20	=D20/C20
21	J. Brown Capital			=B21-C21	=D21/C21
22	Total Liab. & Equity	=SUM(B18:B21)	=SUM(C18:C21)	=B22-C22	=D22/C22

Using the figures from your text, enter the values into the appropriate cells. As you fill in each value the formulas will calculate automatically. Some cells will display a series of pound (#) symbols but they will be replaced by the correct figures as you finish entering all the data.

One last adjustment must be made to the percent column (column E). We need to increase the decimals to two decimal places. Click on the letter E at the top of column E. Now click TWICE on the INCREASE DECIMALS button.

More about Financial Statements

There are largely four major types of financial statements, namely Balance Sheet, Income & Expenses Statement (or simply Income Statement), Cash Flow Statement, and Retained Earnings Statement. These statements are usually updated and reported quarterly. Any publicly traded company must disclose these statements to public - their current or prospective investors (shareholders & stakeholders in general) - at least once a year in the annual report, and file an annual 10K report, which is a kind of annual report, with the SEC. Some firms also file 10Q report quarterly.

1. Balance Sheet

A typical balance sheet consists of two aspects of the financial make-up of a firm: Assets vs. Liabilities & Equity. When a firm starts up, it needs start-up capital or initial investment. How the founding members of the firm raise that capital depends on the fund availability.

The capital thus raised can be used to rent, lease or purchase office equipment, the building for offices & plant, company vehicles, operating expenses during the start-up period including the lead time[1]... etc – *i.e.* they invest all of it initially in the business. If you purchased these items, they are your (the firm's) property, and will be valued at their purchase prices. They will be entered into the record (the book or the balance sheet) initially at these values, hence referred to as book value.[2] These items are also called assets as they will be asset to your business that will be used to generate income for you.

a. Balance Sheet Items

Balance sheet is mainly divided into two sides, Assets vs. Liabilities & Equity. Under each of these categories, line items are listed in the order of liquidity.[3] The assets side shows what asset form the initial infusion of capital is held in – *i.e.* how it got used. The liabilities & equity-side shows where that initial capital came from.

The assets side usually consists of all the liquid assets starting with cash and all the physical assets such as equipment (production and/or office), buildings (plants and/or offices), land... etc. In the above example, liquid assets are also labeled "Current Assets" which also include inventory. Inventory in general is not liquid by its inherent nature, but is considered part of current asset in the sense that it normally doesn't take as much time as such physical assets as land or buildings (Non-Current Assets) to liquidate. After all, if the firm is having a cash flow problem, the firm will try to stave it off by liquidating its current assets – *i.e.* it tries to convert whatever it can into cash to meet the payment obligation that caused this cash shortage in the first place. Stocks, bonds, notes will be sold for cash, and accounts receivable can also be sold at discount[4]. If it still doesn't meet the cash need, the firm will even start selling its physical assets after liquidating inventory.[5]

The liabilities & equity side consists of all the liquid-type liabilities first, physical or non-liquid type, and finally owner's equity[6]. The liquid types are called Current Liabilities, and the non-liquid types are called Non-Current Liabilities. The current liabilities generally consist of short-term debt obligations the firm has created through sale of these debt instrument issues. The non-current liabilities consist of long-term debts the firm incurred through bank loans, private placements, or bond issues usually publicly traded in the established bond exchange.

In building the above balance sheet table, it is important to understand that one only needs initial data set, not all, to begin with – *i.e.* the subtotals and totals don't need to be manually entered. These data, of course, are basically collected from the firm's books & journals. For example, let's assume that we are given only some initial data to begin with as in the following table. This means some data may be missing.

This table would be a more realistic picture of what one might encounter right after the data have just been gathered from the firm's bookkeeping record, and entered into the spreadsheet. It is obvious at a

---

[1] A period of only incurring expenses until their first batch of products gets sold and brings in revenue & some profit

[2] Of course, as time passes, the book value of these assets will be depreciated to reflect the general wear & tear over time. Also, the actual valuation of these assets in the resale market may be different from their book values.

[3] Liquidity refers to the ease with which assets can be converted into cash. *i.e.* how easily one can convert an asset into cash.

[4] This activity is called factoring, and will be discussed further in the chapter about Simple Interest & Bank Discount.

[5] There are industrial bargain buyers called liquidators that source those firms that need to get rid of its old inventory or even the still new inventory due to cash flow issues.

[6] Equity is also called frequently Net Worth especially when the assets and liabilities involve mostly financial types.

glance that the subtotal cells and the total cells are blank and still to be filled in. These cells are highlighted in colors, meaning that they are to be solved for. Of course, in real practice, these cells won't necessarily be highlighted, but it would be visually helpful to highlight them for instructional purpose.

Now, finding the solution for these blanks is a fairly straightforward and easy exercise with Excel. There are several ways one can obtain the solution for this summation problem as follows.

i) Excel has a feature called "Autosum" denoted by the summation symbol "Σ"[7] in the tool bar. The toolbars may be expanded or collapsed depending on the MS Office version, and hence, the icon may be hidden, but in any case one can easily locate it by clicking on the double arrow tip of the toolbar. Once the "Σ" icon is located, then move the cursor to the last cell, where the summed result should be entered, at the bottom of the data string to be summed up. Then, click on the "Σ" icon, *et Voila*! The result is automatically computed. (See Fig II.A.1.c. Autosum)

	A	B	C	D
1	Fig II.A.1.a. Balance Sheet			
2			Percentage	
3	**Current Assets**			
4	Cash	$ 48,000.00		
5	Accouts Receivable	$ 98,000.00		
6	Inventroy	$ 116,000.00		
7	**Total Current Assets**			
8				
9	**Non-Current Assets**			
10	Land	$ 164,000.00		
11	Building	$ 247,600.00		
12	Equipment	$ 131,400.00		
13	**Total Non-Current Assets**			
14	**Total Assets**	$		

Microsoft Excel - Financial Statements
File Edit View Insert Format Tools Data Window Help
B7 =
AutoSum

Prof. Hong:
Place the cursor on this cell, locate and click the summation icon as shown above.

ii) You can also perform the same operation step by step using basic Excel commands. Place the cursor on the target cell to enter the summed result. Enter equal sign "=". Once you enter the equal sign, Excel shifts into the formula mode. That is to say, that Excel expects a mathematical expression in the cell. Now enter the Excel command "sum" followed by a parenthesis, so that the cell would now have an expression "=sum( )" in it. The interpretation of this expression is that the data in the current cell is the sum of certain values. Now, it's time to designate the cells that contain values to go in the parenthesis. The values to fill the parenthesis are contained in a range of data, so we will designate that range. To do this, move the cursor to the first cell in the contiguous range of data in a column or in a row to highlight the data range to sum. (See Figs II.A.1.d. & e.)

iii) Last but not least, the crude, no-frill but straightforward way to do it is quite intuitive and fail-safe. Place the cursor on the cell to enter the sum. Enter "=" and all the cell numbers to

---

[7] It is a mathematical convention to use capitalized Greek character "sigma" to represent summation for the phonetic parallel between the Greek & Roman alphabets.

sum with "+" in between. In this example, to find the solution for Total Current Assets, enter "=b4+b5+b6" in the solution cell b7, and you will obtain the same result as in ii) and iii). (See Fig II.A.1.f.)

	Microsoft Excel - Financial Statements			
	File Edit View Insert Format Tools Data Window Help			
		Σ ↕ 〽 〞 Create PDF	Times New Roman ▾ 12 ▾	
B4	▾ = 48000			
	A	B	C	D
1	Fig II.A.1.a. Balance Sheet			
2			Percentage	
3	**Current Assets**			
4	Cash	$ 48,000.00		
5	Accouts Receivable	$ 98,000.00		
6	Inventroy	$ 116,000.00		
7	**Total Current Assets**			
8				
9	**Non-Current Assets**			
10	Land	$ 164,000.00		
11	Building	$ 247,600.00		
12	Equipment	$ 131,400.00		
13	**Total Non-Current Assets**			
14	**Total Assets**	$		

Prof. Hong:
When the cursor turns from an arrow to a thick white cross, it means Excel is ready to highlight a range. Simply drag it down to the last cell of the range you want to sum.

Designating a range to sum data & clicking on green "Enter" checkmark

	Microsoft Excel - Financial Statements			
	File Edit View Insert Format Tools Data Window Help			
		Σ ↕ 〽 〞 Create PDF	Times New Roman ▾ 12 ▾	
SUM	▾ X ✓ = =SUM(B4:B6)			
	A	B	C	D
1	Fig II.A.1.a. Bala Enter heet			
2			Percentage	
3	**Current Assets**			
4	Cash	$ 48,000.00		
5	Accouts Receivable	$ 98,000.00		
6	Inventroy	$ 116,000.00		
7	**Total Current Assets**	=SUM(B4:B6)		
8				
9	**Non-Current Assets**			
10	Land	$ 164,000.00		
11	Building	$ 247,600.00		
12	Equipment	$ 131,400.00		
13	**Total Non-Current Assets**			
14	**Total Assets**	$ 262,000.00		

Prof. Hong:
Enter "=sum(", and highlight the range of data to sum, and then close the parenthesis ")". Hit enter key or click on the green check mark in the formula bar.

Summing the data mathematically

Microsoft Excel - Financial Statements

File Edit View Insert Format Tools Data Window Help

	AVERAGE	X ✓ =	=B4+B5+B6		
	A	B	C	D
1	Fig II.A.1.f. Summing the data mathematically			
2			Percentage	
3	**Current Assets**			
4	Cash	$ 48,000.00		
5	A.R.	$ 98,000.00		
6	Inventroy	$ 116,000.00		
7	**Total C.A.**	=B4+B5+B6		
8				

Therefore, managing the balance sheet is made a lot easier and routinized that would otherwise have been a tedious number crunching. It saves you trouble of constantly making sure all the numbers are right. If there was any data entry error, the result can be instantly adjusted once you single out only the wrong data and update it. Just keep track of the record for any change in data until the next update, and you will always have an automatically adjusting statement that is accurate and correct to any degree you set it up to.

b. Horizontal and Vertical Analysis

As the firm operates through time, the management wants to know how well it has performed and where it stands. In terms of growth or decline in the size of the firm on annual basis, this can be easily achieved by comparing the balance sheets over a two-year period.

	A	B	C	D	E	F	G
31	**Fig II.C.1.a Horizontal Analysis**						
32				Increase (Decrease)		%	
33		2004	2003	Amount	%	2004	2003
34	Current Assets						
35	Cash	$ 10,000.00	$ 12,000.00	$ (2,000.00)	-17%	7%	9%
36	Securites	$ 5,000.00	$ 3,000.00	$ 2,000.00	67%	3%	2%
37	A.R.	$ 32,000.00	$ 26,000.00	$ 6,000.00	23%	21%	19%
38	Inventory	$ 18,000.00	$ 22,000.00	$ (4,000.00)	-18%	12%	16%
39	Total C.A.	$ 65,000.00	$ 63,000.00	$ 2,000.00	3%	43%	47%
40	Non-Current Assets						
41	Land	$ 38,000.00	$ 38,000.00	$ -	0%	25%	28%
42	Bldg	$ 26,000.00	$ 16,000.00	$ 10,000.00	63%	17%	12%
43	Equip	$ 21,000.00	$ 18,000.00	$ 3,000.00	17%	14%	13%
44	Total Non-C.A.	$ 85,000.00	$ 72,000.00	$ 13,000.00	18%	57%	53%
45	Total Assets	$ 150,000.00	$ 135,000.00	$ 15,000.00	11%	100%	100%
46							
47	Current Liab						
48	A.P.	$ 22,000.00	$ 20,000.00	$ 2,000.00	10%	15%	15%
49	Notes Payable	$ 10,000.00	$ 12,000.00	$ (2,000.00)	-17%	7%	9%
50	Total C.L.	$ 32,000.00	$ 32,000.00	$ -	0%	21%	24%
51	Non-Current Liab						
52	Mortgage	$ 56,500.00	$ 57,000.00	$ (500.00)	-1%	38%	43%
53	Bonds Payable	$ 24,000.00	$ 26,000.00	$ (2,000.00)	-8%	16%	19%
54	Total Non-C.L.	$ 80,500.00	$ 83,000.00	$ (2,500.00)	-3%	54%	62%
55	Total Liab	$ 112,500.00	$ 115,000.00	$ (2,500.00)	-2%	75%	86%
56							
57	Equity	$ 37,500.00	$ 19,000.00	$ 18,500.00	97%	25%	14%
58							
59	Total Liab + Equity	$ 150,000.00	$ 134,000.00	$ 16,000.00	12%	100%	100%

This is usually called "horizontal analysis"[8], as one can check side by side the change in the same line item over time. It may be also considered a kind of "comparative statics" to borrow the terminology from economics, because what it does is to compare the status of the firm between two static points in time. No matter what you may call it, the important thing to remember is that all you need is the initial data set, not the entire set of numbers, to build this table. *i.e.* you are not just entering the raw data and the results calculated elsewhere manually and tediously. The idea is that you only sow the data seed and make Excel do all the rest. The above table is simply a finished product, and would not look, at the beginning, as it appears now. So, let's start at the very beginning.

i) First, we need initial data set compiled from the book periodically. This does not mean in the least that this step must be done only manually. Once we network everything into a database system, all the raw data gathered periodically will be entered directly from the source into the system, automatically linking and updating the data we need constantly. In the absence of such a system, however, we will have to manually enter only the initial data into the table.

	Fig II.C.1.b Horizontal Analysis - Initial Data			Increase (Decrease)		%	
		2004	2003	Amount	%	2004	2003
4	Current Assets						
5	Cash	$ 10,000.00	$ 12,000.00				
6	Securites	$ 5,000.00	$ 3,000.00				
7	A.R.	$ 32,000.00	$ 26,000.00				
8	Inventory	$ 18,000.00	$ 22,000.00				
9	Total C.A.						
10	Non-Current Assets						
11	Land	$ 38,000.00	$ 38,000.00				
12	Bldg	$ 26,000.00	$ 16,000.00				
13	Equip	$ 21,000.00	$ 18,000.00				
14	Total Non-C.A.						
15	Total Assets						
16							
17	Current Liab						
18	A.P.	$ 22,000.00	$ 20,000.00				
19	Notes Payable	$ 10,000.00	$ 12,000.00				
20	Total C.L.						
21	Non-Current Liab						
22	Mortgage	$ 56,500.00	$ 57,000.00				
23	Bonds Payable	$ 24,000.00	$ 26,000.00				
24	Total Non-C.L.						
25	Total Liab						
26							
27	Equity	$ -	$ 19,000.00				
28							
29	Total Liab + Equity	$ -	$ 19,000.00				

As you can see, the initial data are already in place, and the line items that need to be solved for are highlighted. These line items are not difficult to solve for at all as they were already covered in section II.A.1.a. Simply by using "autosum" command, you will be able to have Excel fill in the blanks instantly.

---

[8] Actually, the last two columns (F and G) are not part of the horizontal analysis, but the vertical analysis that will be discussed later.

Microsoft Excel - Financial Statements

File Edit View Insert Format Tools Data Window Help

STDEV X ✓ = =SUM(B⁻ᴮ⁰) AutoSum

	A	B	C	D
1	**Fig II.C.1.c Horizontal Analysis - Fill in the Blanks**			
2				Increase (Dec
3		2004	2003	Amount
4	Current Assets			
5	Cash	$ 10,000.00	$ 12,000.00	
6	Securites	$ 5,000.00	$ 3,000.00	
7	A.R.	$ 32,000.00	$ 26,000.00	
8	Inventory	$ 18,000.00	$ 22,000.00	
9	Total C.A.	=SUM(B5:B8)		
10	Non-Current Assets			
11	Land	$ 38,000.00	$ 38,000.00	
12	Bldg	$ 26,000.00	$ 16,000.00	
13	Equip	$ 21,000.00	$ 18,000.00	
14	Total Non-C.A.			
15	Total Assets			
16				

ii) The rest of the blank line items can be filled also in the same way. Instead of hitting "autosum" every time, you may also use "copy and drag" to find the solution for the adjacent cell. *i.e.* copy and drag the formula in the cell "Total Current Assets" (TCA hereafter) for 2004 into 2003. "Total Assets" (TA hereafter), by definition, can be found by summing TCA and TNCA. *However, you may not simply autosum everything, because there are already subtotals (TCA and TNCA) in the column. An "autosum" will simply double-count all the items.* Therefore, it is absolutely necessary to evaluate critically the operation you are performing, and not to follow it just mechanically. No matter how sophisticated the software, it eventually behooves on every individual that implements the program to make sure that the program is executing the correct set of operations.

STDEV X ✓ = =SUM(B9,B14)

	A	B	C	D
1	**Fig II.C.1.d Horizontal Analysis - Solving for Totals**			
2				Increase (Dec
3		2004	2003	Amount
4	Current Assets			
5	Cash	$ 10,000.00	$ 12,000.00	
6	Securites	$ 5,000.00	$ 3,000.00	
7	A.R.	$ 32,000.00	$ 26,000.00	
8	Inventory	$ 18,000.00	$ 22,000.00	
9	Total C.A.	$ 65,000.00	$ 63,000.00	
10	Non-Current Assets			
11	Land	$ 38,000.00	$ 38,000.00	
12	Bldg	$ 26,000.00	$ 16,000.00	
13	Equip	$ 21,000.00	$ 18,000.00	
14	Total Non-C.A.	$ 85,000.00	$ 72,000.00	
15	Total Assets	=SUM(B9,B14)		
16				

iii) You can do the same to the liabilities side for both 2004 and 2003. You may also copy and paste, but this will work only if the number of line items on both sides is the same. However, we have a small problem with the equity for 2004, because the data is not given.

	A	B	C	D
1	Fig II.C.1.e Horizontal Analysis - Solving for missing value			
2				Increase (De
3		2004	2003	Amount
16				
17	Current Liab			
18	A.P.	$ 22,000.00	$ 20,000.00	
19	Notes Payable	$ 10,000.00	$ 12,000.00	
20	Total C.L.	$ 32,000.00	$ 32,000.00	
21	Non-Current Liab			
22	Mortgage	$ 56,500.00	$ 57,000.00	
23	Bonds Payable	$ 24,000.00	$ 26,000.00	
24	Total Non-C.L.	$ 80,500.00	$ 83,000.00	
25	Total Liab	$ 112,500.00	$ 115,000.00	
26				
27	Equity		$ 19,000.00	
28				
29	Total Liab + Equity			
30				

So, what do we do to find the equity? We have a clue here. By definition, the "Total Liabilities + Equity" (TL+E hereafter) must be equal to the "Total Assets"(TA hereafter), so we have this item already solved for. Therefore, all you need to do is to make a reference to the cell for TA in TL+E cell, and then put the difference between the TL+E and the TL in the "Equity" cell. The rest of the line items for 2003 can be solved in the same way, or you may also enter "=sum(c25,c27)" in c29 for TL+E.

STDEV ▾ ✕ ✓ = =B15

	A	B	C	D
1	Fig II.C.1.f Horizontal Analysis - Solving for missing value			
2				Increase (De
3		2004	2003	Amount
15	Total Assets	$ 150,000.00	$ 135,000.00	
16				
17	Current Liab			
18	A.P.	$ 22,000.00	$ 20,000.00	
19	Notes Payable	$ 10,000.00	$ 12,000.00	
20	Total C.L.	$ 32,000.00	$ 32,000.00	
21	Non-Current Liab			
22	Mortgage	$ 56,500.00	$ 57,000.00	
23	Bonds Payable	$ 24,000.00	$ 26,000.00	
24	Total Non-C.L.	$ 80,500.00	$ 83,000.00	
25	Total Liab	$ 112,500.00	$ 115,000.00	
26				
27	Equity	=B29-B25	$ 19,000.00	
28				
29	Total Liab + Equity	=B15		
30				

iv) Now, the next column is the comparative statics. The columns D and E will show the change – increase or decrease in both dollar amount and percentage – in these line items over time (1-year period to be exact). It is an accounting convention to put the negative numbers in parenthesis or in red to represent the negative change or decrease in value. Excel is preset to use parenthesis or red font by default although you may also set it to use minus sign.

To find the change in dollars, all you need to do is subtract 2003 data from 2004 data after "= sign" for just the first row to begin with. Once the computed result appears in the target cell, then copy, drag and paste it down the column. To find the change in percentage[9], divide the result obtained in the previous operation (change in dollars) by the line item in the previous year. This is because the previous year's value is the base of the change.

Finally, as a cosmetic step, clean the cells that contain no data such as d10, d16, d17, d20, d21, d26, and d28. They are actually blank cells that contain no data, but accidentally picked up a hitchhiker ($ sign) in the process of copy-drag-&-paste. If you don't want the nuisance, do not copy & drag, but just copy & paste only where necessary.

	Fig II.C.1.g Horizontal Analysis - Change over Time				
1					
2				Increase (Decrease)	
3		2004	2003	Amount	%
4	Current Assets				
5	Cash	$ 10,000.00	$ 12,000.00	=B5-C5	=D5/C5
6	Securites	$ 5,000.00	$ 3,000.00	$ 2,000.00	66.67%
7	A.R.	$ 32,000.00	$ 26,000.00	$ 6,000.00	23.08%
8	Inventory	$ 18,000.00	$ 22,000.00	$ (4,000.00)	-18.18%
9	Total C.A.	$ 65,000.00	$ 63,000.00	$ 2,000.00	3.17%
10	Non-Current Assets			$ -	
11	Land	$ 38,000.00	$ 38,000.00	$ -	0.00%
12	Bldg	$ 26,000.00	$ 16,000.00	$ 10,000.00	62.50%
13	Equip	$ 21,000.00	$ 18,000.00	$ 3,000.00	16.67%
14	Total Non-C.A.	$ 85,000.00	$ 72,000.00	$ 13,000.00	18.06%
15	Total Assets	$ 150,000.00	$ 135,000.00	$ 15,000.00	11.11%
16					
17	Current Liab				
18	A.P.	$ 22,000.00	$ 20,000.00	$ 2,000.00	10.00%
19	Notes Payable	$ 10,000.00	$ 12,000.00	$ (2,000.00)	-16.67%
20	Total C.L.	$ 32,000.00	$ 32,000.00	$ -	0.00%
21	Non-Current Liab				
22	Mortgage	$ 56,500.00	$ 57,000.00	$ (500.00)	-0.88%
23	Bonds Payable	$ 24,000.00	$ 26,000.00	$ (2,000.00)	-7.69%
24	Total Non-C.L.	$ 80,500.00	$ 83,000.00	$ (2,500.00)	-3.01%
25	Total Liab	$ 112,500.00	$ 115,000.00	$ (2,500.00)	-2.17%
26					
27	Equity	$ 37,500.00	$ 20,000.00	$ 17,500.00	87.50%
28					
29	Total Liab + Equity	$ 150,000.00	$ 135,000.00	$ 15,000.00	11.11%

v) Let's have a brief overview of this horizontal analysis. Over a year period, TA increased 11.11%. This also means its counterpart (TL+E) has also increased by equal amount. This is definitely a good sign, because it means that the firm grew by as much. It is all the more a

---

[9] This is the basic concept for the net growth rate.

happy news because this growth is mainly due to 87.5% growth in equity. On the other hand, the TL rather decreased by 2.17%. Put two and two together, one can easily understand that the firm's growth is due to good business, and that at least based solely on this one-year horizontal analysis, this was certainly a viable business for the given year. You can expand this type of evaluation to the rest of the line items.

vi) Now, let's move on to the vertical analysis. Vertical analysis refers to finding the proportion of each line item in the composition of the total entirety in a given year. Therefore, it expresses each line item as a fraction of the TA or TL&E, and helps us evaluate if any particular item is in optimal proportion. Of course, this type of judgment is rather discretionary although there is a general rule of thumb for the sector or the industry average. The figure below demonstrates vertical analysis. The concept as well as the technique is simple.

	A	B	C	D	E	F	G
1	Fig II.C.1.h Vertical Analysis - Fraction of Line Items out of the Total						
2				Increase (Decrease)		%	
3		2004	2003	Amount	%	2004	2003
4	Current Assets						
5	Cash	$ 10,000.00	$ 12,000.00	$ (2,000.00)	-16.67%	=B5/B$15	
6	Securites	$ 5,000.00	$ 3,000.00	$ 2,000.00	66.67%	3.33%	
7	A.R.	$ 32,000.00	$ 26,000.00	$ 6,000.00	23.08%	21.33%	
8	Inventory	$ 18,000.00	$ 22,000.00	$ (4,000.00)	-18.18%	12.00%	
9	Total C.A.	$ 65,000.00	$ 63,000.00	$ 2,000.00	3.17%	43.33%	
10	Non-Current Assets						
11	Land	$ 38,000.00	$ 38,000.00	$ -	0.00%	25.33%	
12	Bldg	$ 26,000.00	$ 16,000.00	$ 10,000.00	62.50%	17.33%	
13	Equip	$ 21,000.00	$ 18,000.00	$ 3,000.00	16.67%	14.00%	
14	Total Non-C.A.	$ 85,000.00	$ 72,000.00	$ 13,000.00	18.06%	56.67%	
15	Total Assets	$ 150,000.00	$ 135,000.00	$ 15,000.00	11.11%	100.00%	
16							
17	Current Liab						
18	A.P.	$ 22,000.00	$ 20,000.00	$ 2,000.00	10.00%	=B18/B$29	
19	Notes Payable	$ 10,000.00	$ 12,000.00	$ (2,000.00)	-16.67%	6.67%	
20	Total C.L.	$ 32,000.00	$ 32,000.00	$ -	0.00%	21.33%	
21	Non-Current Liab					0.00%	
22	Mortgage	$ 56,500.00	$ 57,000.00	$ (500.00)	-0.88%	37.67%	
23	Bonds Payable	$ 24,000.00	$ 26,000.00	$ (2,000.00)	-7.69%	16.00%	
24	Total Non-C.L.	$ 80,500.00	$ 83,000.00	$ (2,500.00)	-3.01%	53.67%	
25	Total Liab	$ 112,500.00	$ 115,000.00	$ (2,500.00)	-2.17%	75.00%	
26						0.00%	
27	Equity	$ 37,500.00	$ 19,000.00	$ 18,500.00	97.37%	25.00%	
28						0.00%	
29	Total Liab + Equity	$ 150,000.00	$ 134,000.00	$ 16,000.00	11.94%	100.00%	

To find the fraction of cash in TA for 2004, enter "=b5/b$15" in the target cell f5. Remember to lock the cell b15 by inserting a "$" sign before 15[10]. It is self-explanatory why we do this. We want to avoid entering the same b15 repeatedly just because all the line items on the asset side need dividing by the TA. Then, move the cursor to the lower right corner of the cell border, wait for the thick white cross to turn into a thin black cross, and drag to copy all the way down to the TA row. Repeat the same process for the liabilities side as well. This time, remember that the denominator of the fraction must be b$29, TL&E. *Et voilà!* You have the vertical analysis for 2004.

---

[10] Actually, since it's only the row that will adjust if left unlocked, not the column as we go down each line item, we need only to lock the row.

vii) For 2003, you will repeat the same process with the 2003 data.

	A	B	C	D	F	G
1	Fig II.C.1.i Vertical Analysis - Collapsing the Columns					
2				(C	%	
3		2004	2003	no	2004	2003
4	Current Assets					
5	Cash	$ 10,000.00	$ 12,000.00		6.67%	=C5/C$15
6	Securites	$ 5,000.00	$ 3,000.00		3.33%	2.22%
7	A.R.	$ 32,000.00	$ 26,000.00		21.33%	19.26%
8	Inventory	$ 18,000.00	$ 22,000.00		12.00%	16.30%
9	Total C.A.	$ 65,000.00	$ 63,000.00		43.33%	46.67%
10	Non-Current Assets					
11	Land	$ 38,000.00	$ 38,000.00		25.33%	28.15%
12	Bldg	$ 26,000.00	$ 16,000.00		17.33%	11.85%
13	Equip	$ 21,000.00	$ 18,000.00		14.00%	13.33%
14	Total Non-C.A.	$ 85,000.00	$ 72,000.00		56.67%	53.33%
15	Total Assets	$ 150,000.00	$ 135,000.00		100.00%	100.00%
16						
17	Current Liab					
18	A.P.	$ 22,000.00	$ 20,000.00		14.67%	=C18/C$29
19	Notes Payable	$ 10,000.00	$ 12,000.00		6.67%	8.96%
20	Total C.L.	$ 32,000.00	$ 32,000.00		21.33%	23.88%
21	Non-Current Liab					
22	Mortgage	$ 56,500.00	$ 57,000.00		37.67%	42.54%
23	Bonds Payable	$ 24,000.00	$ 26,000.00		16.00%	19.40%
24	Total Non-C.L.	$ 80,500.00	$ 83,000.00		53.67%	61.94%
25	Total Liab	$ 112,500.00	$ 115,000.00		75.00%	85.82%
26						
27	Equity	$ 37,500.00	$ 19,000.00		25.00%	14.18%
28						
29	Total Liab + Equity	$ 150,000.00	$ 134,000.00		100.00%	100.00%

This time, since we are dealing with vertical analysis for 2003 only, the columns that were used for horizontal analysis are not immediately needed, and hence, may be collapsed to hide some columns to save the space. This is done by simply placing the cursor on the border between the two column labels such as E and F, and when the cursor turns into a thin black cross with two-way arrow arm, dragging the border line left until columns D and E are completely eclipsed by the column F. One can easily tell whether the firm had unusually high cash position or not in 2003…*etc.*

viii) As a general rule, we use only up to two decimal places – *i.e.* round up to the nearest hundredth – for the consistency in the format. This can be done simply by highlighting the entire table and clicking on the decimals icon on the toolbar to the desired level.

| Arial | | 12 | | B *I* U | | | | | $ % , | | | | |

Increase Decimal

D	E	F	G	H
Fig II.C.1.j Vertical Analysis - Setting Decimal Levels				
Increase (Decrease)		%		
Amount	%	2004	2003	
$ (2,000.00)	-16.67%	6.67%	8.89%	
$ 2,000.00	66.67%	3.33%	2.22%	
$ 6,000.00	23.08%	21.33%	19.26%	
$ (4,000.00)	-18.18%	12.00%	16.30%	
$ 2,000.00	3.17%	43.33%	46.67%	
$ -	0.00%	25.33%	28.15%	
$ 10,000.00	62.50%	17.33%	11.85%	
$ 3,000.00	16.67%	14.00%	13.33%	
$ 13,000.00	18.06%	56.67%	53.33%	
$ 15,000.00	11.11%	100.00%	100.00%	

2. Income & Expenses Statement

We now move on to the Income & Expenses Statement or simply Income Statement for short. The income statement shows all the sources of income and the uses thereof (expenses). One must not confuse Income Statement and Balance Sheet. The balance sheet is not about how much money a firm makes, but about how it raised capital and what asset forms they are held in, whereas the income statement is all about how much money (gross income) the firm brings in, how much it spends, and hence, how much profit (net income) it ends up with. It is reported quarterly as well as annually, but the data are collected and compiled constantly for internal managerial purposes.

a. Two-Step Profit Statement

	A6	=	
	A	B	C
1	**Fig II.A.2.a Income Statement**		
2			%
3	Gross Rev	$ 1,030,000.00	103%
4	Returns & Allowances	$ (30,000.00)	-3%
5	**Net Rev**	$ 1,000,000.00	100%
6			
7	Beg Inventory	$ 92,000.00	
8	Purchase	$ 665,000.00	
9	Returns & Allowances	$ (23,500.00)	
10	GAS	$ 733,500.00	
11	End Inventory	$ (83,500.00)	
12	**Total CGS**	$ 650,000.00	65%
13			
14	**Gross Profit**	$ 350,000.00	35%
15			
16	Salaries	$ 90,000.00	9%
17	Rent	$ 18,000.00	2%
18	Utilities	$ 8,000.00	1%
19	Admin	$ 23,500.00	2%
20	Depreciation	$ 20,500.00	2%
21	**Total Oper Expenses**	$ 160,000.00	16%
22			
23	**Operating Income**	$ 190,000.00	19%
24			
25	Taxes	$ 90,000.00	9%
26			
27	**Net Profit**	$ 100,000.00	10%

The above is an example of one type of Income Statement. We will call the following format "Two-Step Profit Statement" or "Type A" for short for the reasons to be discussed below.

Once again, those highlighted areas were not given to begin with, and need to be solved for, which will be discussed later in this section. First, as a matter of convention, most accounting practices would follow two-column table which places all the "money-ins" (income) in one column and all the "money-outs"(expenses) in the next column, but we will use a single column format for ease of computation. Let's review each line item by broader groups.

i) The first line item is the "Gross Revenue", which is the sales revenue before any adjustments. The adjustments are mainly "Returns" – *i.e.* all the goods returned for which refund was made, and hence, a minus item from your income list – and "Allowances", discounts the firm gave to the customers or the distribution channel members, also a minus item from your income list. Then, there is usually an investment income[11] item, which is not the case with this firm. When all these line items are summed up, then the "Net Revenue" is obtained.

STDEV	▾ X ✓ =	=SUM(B3:B4)		
	A	B	C	D
1	Fig II.A.2.a.i Finding Net Revenue			
2			%	
3	Gross Rev	$ 1,030,000.00	=B3/B$5	
4	Returns & Allowances	$ (30,000.00)	-3.00%	
5	Net Rev	=SUM(B3:B4)	100.00%	
6				
7	Beg Inventory	Prof. Hong: Since Returns & Allowances are already in negative, Just sum b3 through b4.	00 Prof. Hong: All line items are expressed in the fractions of the Net Rev. Therefore, lock the cell to keep b5 as the base for all the fractions.	
8	Purchase		00	
9	Returns & Allowance		00	
10	GAS	$ 733,500.00		
11	End Inventory	$ (83,500.00)		
12	Total CGS	$ 650,000.00	65.00%	
13				
14	Gross Profit	$ 350,000.00	35.00%	

ii) Then, as we move down to the "Expenses Account", the first item is the "Beginning Inventory". However, you need to look past this item to see the big picture, because the first major expenses item is the "Cost of Goods Sold" (Total CGS), not the "Begin Inventory". Regardless of the type of business – manufacture or retail, firms must sell goods to bring in income. When a manufacturer produces goods, they do not know with accuracy how many units will be sold, so their target production level may overshoot or undershoot the actual sales level. The production cost may vary in each case, but as long as they sell some quantity, it brings in revenue or income.[12] Lines A7 through A11 show how this Total CGS is obtained:

a) The firm starts a month or a quarter with the beginning inventory (A7), which is actually the ending inventory of goods carried over from the previous period.

---

[11] The investment income is the realized capital gains or dividend payouts from stocks, interest payments from bonds, commercial papers, CDs and/or from investing in any other financial instruments. The above table doesn't show any investment income, as the firm didn't have any.
[12] The term revenue is basically the same thing as income, and hence, these two terms are used interchangeably. So are the terms cost and expenses. Also, the term "net income" is used interchangeably with "net profit".

b) This may not be sufficient to meet the expected sales for the current period, so the firm places a new purchase order (A8) with its supplier (distributor or vendor).

c) Some of these new orders may be defective or wrong item, so the firm returns them or gets some discounts (A9).

d) Then, the sum of these three items makes the "Goods Available for Sale" (A10 GAS), and all the goods they sold during the period make the Total CGS (A12).

e) So, by definition GAS less CGS will give "Ending Inventory" (A11).

f) Logically, End Inventory follows CGS, but for our purpose, the example switched the order so that we can end the analysis of our first major expense item with CGS. In this case, the End Inventory must be subtracted from the GAS to arrive at CGS.

	STDEV ▾ ✗ ✓ = =SUM(B7:B9)			
	A	B	C	
1	Fig II.A.2.a.ii Finding Cost of Goods Sold			
2			%	
3	Gross Rev	$	Prof. Hong:	)%
4	Returns & Allowances	$	So long as there are goods left unsold, Ending Inventory is not negative, but	)%
5	**Net Rev**	$	only expressed as negative to simplify the process of finding the CGS.	)%
6				
7	Beg Inventory	$ 92,000.00		
8	Purchase	$ 665,000.00		
9	Returns & Allowances	$ (23,500.00)		
10	GAS	=SUM(B7:B9)		
11	End Inventory	$ (83,500.00)		
12	**Total CGS**	=SUM(B10:B11)	=B12/B$5	
13				
14	**Gross Profit**	=B5-B12	35.00%	
15				

iii) From i) Net Revenue, if we subtract ii) Cost of Goods Sold, we get the Gross Profit. It is not the real profit yet since there are still expenses that are not directly related to production or procurement of goods, but simply with administrative/ operational aspect of the firm.

iv) These Other Expenses or Operating Expenses are such expenses as Salaries, Rent, Utilities, Administrative, and Depreciation... etc.

v) Subtracting v) Total Other Expenses form iv) Gross Profit, we arrive at Operating Income. Only now are we free from any expenses.

vi) However, we are not yet free from Interest Payments to the outstanding loans or bonds that we have as part of our liabilities, nor from Taxes. Fortunately, our sample firm doesn't owe any interest payments.

vii) Subtracting vii) Interests and Taxes from vi) Operating Income, we finally arrive at the "Net Profit".

	STDEV ▾	X ✓ =	=SUM(B16:B20)	

	A	B	C
1	Fig II.A.2.a.iii Operating Expenses/ Operating Income		
15			
16	Salaries	$ 90,000.00	9.00%
17	Rent	$ 18,000.00	1.80%
18	Utilities	$ 8,000.00	0.80%
19	Admin	$ 23,500.00	2.35%
20	Depreciation	$ 20,500.00	2.05%
21	Total Oper Expenses	=SUM(B16:B20)	=B21/B$5
22			
23	Operating Income	=B14-B21	=B23/B$5
24			
25	Taxes	$ 90,000.00	9.00%
26			
27	Net Profit	=B23-B25	10.00%
28			

b. Income Statement Practice

Now, let's have a hands-on number-crunching experience with income statement. The following table is a simulation that contains only some data with the rest missing. Your job is to piece together the puzzle and find the missing values.

i) At a first glance, you might be clueless as to what should be the net revenue much less the gross revenue. You simply don't seem to have enough data. However, if you look a few rows down, you will see TTL CGS and Gross Profit. Now, as Gross Profit = Net Rev – TTL CGS, you can figure out Net Rev = Gross Profit + TTL CGS.

ii) Once you've found Net Rev, then Gross Sale (Gross Rev) is automatic. Since Gross Rev – Returns = Net Rev and you have data for Net Rev and Returns, Gross Rev = Net Rev + Returns. Keep in mind, however, that Returns in already in negative, so if you add them up, it will be like subtracting Returns from Net Rev. To prevent it, you'll need to put a minus sign before Returns, and enter "=b4-b3" in b2, and *Voilà* the Gross Sales.

iii) The next line item is Purchase, which can be obtained by subtracting Begin Inventory and Returns & Allowances from Goods Available for Sale. However, GAS data is not available yet, so this item cannot be solved for just yet. However, the following clues now emerge as we move on to solve for GAS.

	Fig II.A.2.b.ii Income Statement Exercise			%	
1					
2	Gross Sales				
3	Returns & allow	$	(72,400.00)		
4	Net Rev			100%	
5					
6	CGS				
7	Beg Inv	$	123,200.00		
8	Purchase				
9	Returns & allow	$	(25,000.00)		
10	GAS				
11	End Inv	$	(137,800.00)		
12	TTL CGS	$	949,000.00		
13					
14	Gross Profit	$	511,000.00		
15					
16	Salaries	$	73,400.00		
17	Depr				
18	Rent	$	25,800.00		
19	Admin	$	24,100.00		
20	Advert	$	46,800.00		
21	Operating Exp			15%	
22					
23	Opera Income				
24					
25	Taxes	$	73,000.00		
26					
27	Net Income				

Fig II.A.2.b.iii Logical Clues

			%
Gross Sales			
Returns & allow	$	(72,400.00)	
Net Rev			100%
CGS			
Beg Inv	$	123,200.00	
Purchase			
Returns & allow	$	(25,000.00)	
GAS			
End Inv	$	(137,800.00)	
TTL CGS	$	949,000.00	
Gross Profit	$	511,000.00	
Salaries	$	73,400.00	
Depr			
Rent	$	25,800.00	
Admin	$	24,100.00	
Advert	$	46,800.00	
Operating Exp			15%
Opera Income			
Taxes	$	73,000.00	
Net Income			

Prof. Hong:
By definition, Gross Rev - Returns = Net Rev
Therefore, Gross = Net Rev + Returns

Prof. Hong:
GAS = B.I. + Purchase - returns
Therefore, Purchase = GAS - (B.I. + Returns)

Prof. Hong:
TTL CGS = GAS - End Inv
Therefore, GAS = TTL CGS + End Inv

Prof. Hong:
Gross Profit = Net Rev - TTL CGS
Therefore, Net Rev = Gross Profit + TTL CGS

Prof. Hong:
Since Oper Exp = 15%*Net Rev.

Prof. Hong:
Operating Income = Gross Profit - Operating Exp

iv) Then, as TTL CGS = GAS – E.I., and we have data for both CGS and End Inventory, now we can solve for GAS = TTL CGS + E.I.

v) Since GAS = B.I. + Purchase – Returns, and we now have data for both GAS and B.I., so Purchase = GAS – (B.I. + Returns). Also, pay attention to the algebraic sign of Returns. It is already negative, so you'll need to make adjustments accordingly as in ii).

vi) Now, we move on to the Expenses. However, the first missing item, depreciation, comes with no immediate clue. Since "b21= sum(b16:b20)", meaning that the operating expenses is the sum of salaries through advertising expenses, we need data for Operating Exp before finding out Depreciation. So, we need to figure out Operating Expenses first.

vii) Fortunately, you have a clue to Operating Exp in the next column. Cell C21 indicates that Operating Exp is 15% of… Net Rev. How do we know it is 15% of Net Rev? Well, 15 out 100%, which is the Net Rev in b4. Now enter "=b4*c21" in b21, and you have the Operating Exp.

viii) Then, Salaries is simply operating exp – sum of all other expenses excluding salaries, which can be solved for by entering "=b21-sum(b16, sum(b18:b20))" in cell b17.

ix) You now have data to solve for Operating Income, which is simply Gross Profit – Operating Expenses.

x) Finally, Net Income = Operating Income – (Interest + Taxes), where interest payment is 0 in our example.

PROBLEM: Using any figures of your own, replace the figures from Problem 16-3 on your spreadsheet.

Chapter 17 Problems

In Problem 4 of the Summary Practice Test we will calculate depreciation and difference between the book value and amount Victor of Prestige.Com received using the straight-line method.

In cell A1 type "Purchase Price".

In cell A2 type "Life Expectancy".

In cell A3 type "Years in Service".

In cell A4 type "Residual (Salvage) Value".

In cell A5 type "Selling (Resale) Price".

In cell A6 type "(Accumulated) Depreciation".

In cell A7 type "Book Value".

In cell A8 type "Difference"

Click on the letter A at the top of column A and then click on the FOMAT menu, highlight COLUMN command and click on AUTOFIT SELECTION.

Next hold down the CONTROL key and click on cells B1, B3, B5, B6, B7, and B8. Now let go of the CONTROL key and click on the CURRENCY button ($). Now you will enter the formulas. If you have any problems you will find the formulas in appendix A.

In cell B6 enter the formula to calculate the straight line figure by taking the purchase price, subtracting the residual value, dividing by the life expectancy and multiplying by the number of years in service (owned).

In cell B7 enter the formula for the book value which is the selling price minus the depreciation.

In cell B8 enter the formula to calculate the difference by taking the book value and subtracting the selling price.

Your spreadsheet should look like this:

	A	B	C
1	Purchae Price		
2	Life Expectancy		
3	Years in Service		
4	Residual (Salvage) Value		
5	Selling (Resale) Price		
6	(Accumulated) Depreciation	#DIV/0!	
7	Book Value	#DIV/0!	
8	Difference	#DIV/0!	
9			

	A	B	C
1	Purchae Price		
2	Life Expectancy		
3	Years in Service		
4	Residual (Salvage) Value		
5	Selling (Resale) Price		
6	(Accumulated) Depreciation	=(B1-B4)/B2*B3	
7	Book Value	=B1-B6	
8	Difference	=B5-B7	
9			

Now enter the values from the problem.

In cell B1 enter the Toyota's purchase price.

In cell B2 enter the life expectancy.

In cell B3 enter the years in service (owned).

In cell B4 enter the residual (salvage) value.

In cell B5 enter the selling (resale) price.

The straight-line depreciation book value is $13,000 and the difference is $6,000.

	A	B	C
1	Purchae Price	$ 28,000.00	
2	Life Expectancy	5.00	
3	Years in Service	3.00	
4	Residual (Salvage) Value	$ 3,000.00	
5	Selling (Resale) Price	$ 19,000.00	
6	(Accumulated) Depreciation	$ 15,000.00	
7	Book Value	$ 13,000.00	
8	Difference	$ 6,000.00	
9			

We can also easily build the depreciation schedule as follows.

	A	B	C	D	E
1	Purchase Price	Salvage Value	Life Expectancy	Annual Deprec	Rate
2	28000	3000	5	=(A2-B2)/C2	=1/C2
3					
4			Depreication Skdl		
5	Years in Srvc	Annual Deprec	Accumul Deprec	Book Value	
6	1	=$D$2	=B6	=$A$2-C6	
7	2	=$D$2	=C6+B7	=$A$2-C7	
8	3	=$D$2	=C7+B8	=$A$2-C8	
9	4	=$D$2	=C8+B9	=$A$2-C9	
10	5	=$D$2	=C9+B10	=$A$2-C10	
11					

Doc J:
Residual (Salvage) Value

Once the given data are entered, then the schedule will automatically be calculated as follows.

	A	B	C	D	E	F
1	Purchase Price	Salvage Value	Life Expectancy	Annual Deprec	Rate	
2	$28,000.00	$3,000.00	5	$5,000.00	20.00%	
3						
4		Depreication Skdl			Doc J: Residual (Salvage) Value	
5	Years in Srvc	Annual Deprec	Accumul Deprec	Book Value		
6	1	$5,000.00	$5,000.00	$23,000.00		
7	2	$5,000.00	$10,000.00	$18,000.00		
8	3	$5,000.00	$15,000.00	$13,000.00		
9	4	$5,000.00	$20,000.00	$8,000.00		
10	5	$5,000.00	$25,000.00	$3,000.00		
11						

PROBLEM: You are a mechanic and buy a tow truck. The cost is $45,000. The life expectancy is 15 years and there is a residual value of $7,500. You sell the truck after 8 years for $15,000. Using the straight-line method what would the difference be between the book value and the selling price?

Chapter 18 Problems

We will do inventory accounting using the Last In, First Out (LIFO) method found in Problem 18-21.

In cell A1 type "LIFO".

In cell A2 type "01/01:".*

In cell A3 type "Quantity:".

In cell A4 type "Cost:".

In cell A5 type "Total:".

In cell A7 type "12/01:".

In cell A8 type "Quantity:".

In cell A9 type "Cost:".

In cell A10 type "Total:".

In cell A12 tyoe "Total Quantity".

In cell A13 type "Total Value:".

In cell A15 type "Quantity Sold".

In cell A16 type "Cost of Goods Slod"

In cell A18 type "Ending Inventory (Q'ty):".

In cell A19 type "Ending Inventory ($):".

	A	B
1	a. LIFO	
2	39083	
3	Quantity:	10
4	Cost:	9
5	Total:	=B3*B4
6		
7	39417	
8	Quantity:	5
9	Cost:	10
10	Total:	=B8*B9
11		
12	Total Quantity:	=SUM(B3,B8)
13	Total Value:	=SUM(B5,B10)
14		
15	Quantity Sold:	7
16	Cost of Goods Sold:	=B13-B19
17		
18	Ending Inventory (Q'ty):	=B12-B15
19	Ending Inventory ($):	=B18*B4

	A	B
1	a. LIFO	
2	1-Jan	
3	Quantity:	10
4	Cost:	$ 9.00
5	Total:	$ 90.00
6		
7	1-Dec	
8	Quantity:	5
9	Cost:	$ 10.00
10	Total:	$ 50.00
11		
12	Total Quantity:	15
13	Total Value:	$ 140.00
14		
15	Quantity Sold:	7.00
16	Cost of Goods Sold:	$ 68.00
17		
18	Ending Inventory (Q'ty):	8.00
19	Ending Inventory ($):	$ 72.00

* If the calendar format is not set as default, click on "Format" on the toolbar, select "Cells", and under the 'Number" tab, select "Date", and select the appropriate date format in the menu box.

We have changed the width of column A by clicking on the FORMAT menu; select COLUMNS; select AUTOWIDTH. You will see by using the centering and right alignment controls you can move the titles to different positions. Now widen column B by clicking on FORMAT; selecting COLUMNS; select WIDTH and type in 16.

Now enter the values from the text. Again, if you have any trouble with the formulas you will find them in Appendix A.

In cell B3 enter the quantity of the first purchase.

In cell B4 enter the cost of those units.

In cell B5 enter the formula to calculate the total.

In cell B8 enter the quantity of the second purchase.

In cell B9 enter the cost.

In cell B10 enter the formula to calculate the total.

In cell B12 enter the formula for total quantity.

In cell B13 enter the formula for total value.

In cell B15 enter the quantity sold.

In cell B16 enter the formula for the cost of goods sold.

In cell B19 enter the quantity of the ending inventory.

In cell B21 enter the formula to calculate the value of ending inventory using the LIFO method.

The solution by FIFO is as follows.

	A	B		A	B
1	b. FIFO		1	b. FIFO	
2	39083		2	1-Jan	
3	Quantity:	10	3	Quantity:	10
4	Cost:	9	4	Cost:	$ 9.00
5	Total:	=B3*B4	5	Total:	$ 90.00
6			6		
7	39417		7	1-Dec	
8	Quantity:	5	8	Quantity:	5
9	Cost:	10	9	Cost:	$ 10.00
10	Total:	=B8*B9	10	Total:	$ 50.00
11			11		
12	Total Quantity:	=SUM(B3,B8)	12	Total Quantity:	15
13	Total Value:	=SUM(B5,B10)	13	Total Value:	$140.00
14			14		
15	Quantity Sold:	7	15	Quantity Sold:	7.00
16	Cost of Goods Sold:	=B13-B19	16	Cost of Goods Sold:	$ 63.00
17			17		
18	Ending Inventory (Q'ty):	=B12-B15	18	Ending Inventory (Q'ty):	8.00
19	Ending Inventory ($):	=B8*B9+(B18-B8)*B4	19	Ending Inventory ($):	$ 77.00

You should have $72 as the cost of the ending inventory in LIFO, and $77 in FIFO.

We can use an alternative method to solve the problem as follows. With this method, one can find inventory values by all three inventory valuation methods (Average cost, FIFO, and LIFO) as well as the resulting Cost of Goods Sold respectively.

E9	▼	=	=C3*D3+(C6-C3)*D2		
	A	B	C	D	E	F
1		Month	Q'ty	U Price	Amount	CGS
2		39814	10	9	=C2*D2	
3		40148	5	10	=C3*D3	
4		GAS	=SUM(C2:C3)	=E4/C4	=SUM(E2:E3)	
5		Q'ty Sold	7	Dr. J:		
6		End Inv	=C4-C5	Weighted AVG price = Total Value of Inventrory / Q'ty		
7		WAVG			=C6*D4	=E4-E7
8	a.	LIFO			=C6*D2	=E4-E8
9	b.	FIFO			=C3*D3+(C6-C3)*D2	=E4-E9

The above model automatically produces the desired solution values in the following table.

E9	▼	=	=C3*D3+(C6-C3)*D2		
	A	B	C	D	E	F
1		Month	Q'ty	U Price	Amount	CGS
2		1-Jan	10	$ 9.00	$ 90.00	
3		1-Dec	5	$ 10.00	$ 50.00	
4		GAS	15	$ 9.33	$ 140.00	
5		Q'ty Sold		Dr. J:		
6		End Inv		Weighted AVG price = Total Value of Inventrory / Q'ty		
7		WAVG			$ 74.67	$ 65.33
8	a.	LIFO			$ 72.00	$ 68.00
9	b.	FIFO			$ 77.00	$ 63.00

PROBLEM: You work for a store that received 15 scented candles at $12.00 each on Monday; 10 scented candles at $25.00 each on Tuesday; 20 scented candles at $15.00 on Wednesday. Calculate your total cost. Now on Thursday you find you have 30 candles left. Calculate the ending inventory and the cost of goods sold using LIFO.

Chapter 19 Problems

We will use problems 4 and 6 from the Summary Practice Test. Before building the table, enter problem numbers in cells A1 and A5 as follows. Enter appropriate labels for each problem in column B. Column widths can be automatically adjusted by double-clicking on the border between column heads.

	A	B	C	D
1	#4	Budget required		
2		TTL Assessed value		
3		Tax rate	#DIV/0!	
4				
5	#6	Market value		
6		Assessment rate		
7		Assessed value	$ –	
8		Tax rate		
9		Property tax	$ –	
10				

Now enter appropriate data and formulas in column B as follows.

	A	B	C	D
1	#4	Budget required	910000	
2		TTL Assessed value	180000000	
3		Tax rate	=C1/C2	
4				
5	#6	Market value	=880000	
6		Assessment rate	0.35	
7		Assessed value	=C5*C6	
8		Tax rate	=0.0589	
9		Property tax	=C7*C8	
10			$18,141.20	

Once the data are filled in, the solutions are automatically obtained.

	A	B	C	D
1	#4	Budget required	$ 910,000.00	
2		TTL Assessed value	$ 180,000,000.00	
3		Tax rate	0.51%	
4				
5	#6	Market value	$ 880,000.00	
6		Assessment rate	35%	
7		Assessed value	$ 308,000.00	
8		Tax rate	5.89%	
9		Property tax	$ 18,141.20	
10				

PROBLEM: Modify the above format accordingly and do problems 3 and 5 in the Summary Practice Test.

Chapter 20 Problems

We will use problems 20-8, 9 and 11. Enter appropriate labels for each problem in column A. Enter appropriate labels for each problem in column A. Column widths can be automatically adjusted by double-clicking on the border between column heads.

	A	B	C	D	E
1			Factor	Doc J: From Table 20.3	
2	Area rating				
3	Bldg class				
4	Property value		$ –	Doc J: From Table 20.3	
5	Contents value		$ –		
6	Annual premium		$ –		
7					
8			Short-rate	Doc J: From Table 20.4	
9	Annual premium				
10	Cancel month				
11	Cost of premium	$ –			
12	Refund	$ –			
13					
14			Factor	Doc J: per Company policy	
15	Replace value				
16	Coinsurance value	$ –			
17	Insured value				
18	Loss				
19	Insurance covers	#DIV/0!	#DIV/0!		
20					

Now enter appropriate data and formulas in column B and C as follows.

One thing to bear in mind is that although the factors by the table are for every $100 or every $1,000 (Life insurance), we would rather use factors for every $1. It won't be too much of a trouble to revert them back to factors $1 basis. (This applies to all factors except the short-rate, which is nothing but a straight-forward %.). All we need to do is simply divide them by 100 or 1,000 accordingly. This way we can put everything back on the level playing field, and not bother any more whether it is a life insurance problem or fire insurance problem.

	A	B	C	D
1			Factor	Doc J: From Table 20.3
2	Area rating	3	0.0061	
3	Bldg class	B	0.0065	
4	Property value	90000	=B4*C2	Doc J: From Table 20.3
5	Contents value	40000	=B5*C3	
6	Annual premium		=SUM(C4:C5)	
7				
8			Short-rate	Doc J: From Table 20.4
9	Annual premium	700		
10	Cancel month	8	0.74	
11	Cost of premium	=B9*C10		
12	Refund	=B9-B11		
13				
14			Factor	Doc J: per Company policy
15	Replace value	100000		
16	Coinsurance value	=B15*C16	0.8	
17	Insured value	60000		
18	Loss	22000		
19	Insurance covers	=B18*C19	=B17/B16	
20				

Once the data are filled in, the solutions are automatically obtained.

	A	B	C	D	E
1			Factor	Doc J: From Table 20.3	
2	Area rating	3	0.610%		
3	Bldg class	B	0.650%		
4	Property value	$ 90,000.00	$ 549.00	Doc J: From Table 20.3	
5	Contents value	$ 40,000.00	$ 260.00		
6	Annual premium		$ 809.00		
7					
8			Short-rate	Doc J: From Table 20.4	
9	Annual premium	$ 700.00			
10	Cancel month	8	74.00%		
11	Cost of premium	$ 518.00			
12	Refund	$ 182.00			
13					
14			Factor	Doc J: per Company policy	
15	Replace value	$ 100,000.00			
16	Coinsurance value	$ 80,000.00	0.8		
17	Insured value	$ 60,000.00			
18	Loss	$ 22,000.00			
19	Insurance covers	$ 16,500.00	0.75		
20					

PROBLEM: Modify the above format accordingly and do problems Practice Quiz 1,2 and 3.

Chapter 21 Problems

We will use problems 21-19. Enter appropriate labels for each problem in column A. Column widths can be automatically adjusted by double-clicking on the border between column heads.

	A	B	C
1	EPS		
2	Price		
3	Dividend		Doc J:
4	P/E	=B2/B1	Earnings per Share
5	Yield	=B3/B2	
6			

Now enter appropriate data and formulas in column B and C as follows.

	A	B	C
1	EPS	4.8	
2	Price	59.25	
3	Dividend	1.4	Doc J:
4	P/E	=B2/B1	Earnings per Share
5	Yield	=B3/B2	
6			

Once the data are filled in, the solutions are automatically obtained.

	A	B	C	D
1	EPS	$ 4.80		
2	Price	$ 59.25		
3	Dividend	$ 1.40	Doc J:	
4	P/E	12.34	Earnings per Share	
5	Yield	2.4%		
6				

Tracking a Stock

What would be the most critical factor in picking a stock? Rate of return, Of course! Then, how do you find the rate of return (or simply return)? Well, if you bought a baseball card for $100, and sold it some time later for $110, you made $10 out of it. That $10, or the proceeds from that sale, is the return, and 10% in %. Why is it 10%? Since the return, $10, is 1/10 of the base ($100), or what you paid for it in the first place. This gives you a simple and straightforward formula for "*r*", the rate of return as follows:

$$r = \frac{Return\ in\ \$}{Price\ paid} = \frac{Price\ @\ point\ of\ sale - Price\ @\ point\ of\ purchase}{Price\ @\ point\ of\ purchase} = \frac{P_t - P_{t-1}}{P_{t-1}}$$

where P_t is the price at current period,
P_{t-1} is the price at previous period.

Originally, the formula should also include "Dividend" in the numerator as $r_t = \dfrac{(P_t - P_{t-1}) - D_t}{P_{t-1}}$, but since we will use "Adjusted Price", which has the effect of dividend payout already incorporated in, it wouldn't matter at all to leave it out of our example.

Let's have an actual hands-on exercise in finding the rate of return. Go to yahoo.com and click on Yahoo Finance. Once you are there, you will see a small window to enter ticker symbol to get the stock quotes. We want to see the price quotes for Microsoft stock, so we enter "msft", which is the symbol for Microsoft. Then you will see the following result.

First, click on the max under the graph to see how the Microsoft has been behaving since it was first listed in the stock exchange.

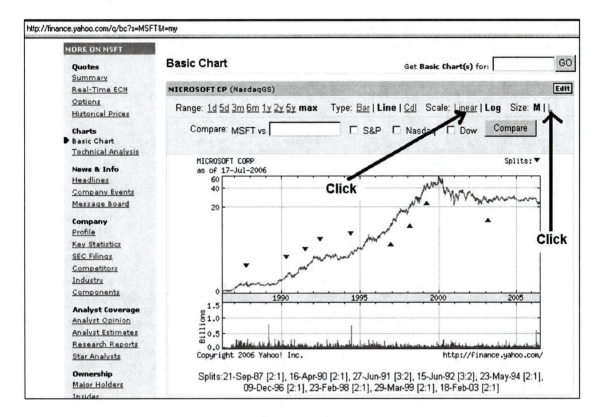

Click on "Linear" for the scale, and "L" for the size, and the graph will appear as follows.

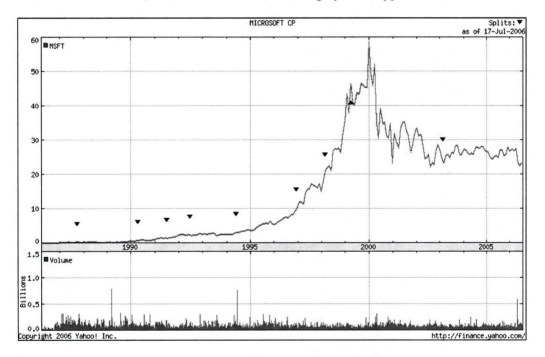

It is visually clear that over ten year period between 1990 and 2000, the stock grew by almost 6,000% even after splits, and even after 2000, the stock is still trading around $20~ $30 range even after several splits, which is still about 2,000~3,000% growth without considering splits.

Now, click on the "Historical Prices" link in the left-hand side panel, and once you are in the new page, select data frequency as monthly, and set the data range to include from Jan 01, 2000 to date, and then click "Get Prices".

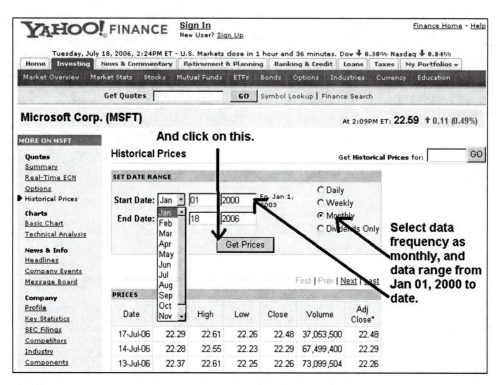

Once you have the desired results, scroll down to the bottom of the screen and click "Download to Spreadsheet". When the dialogue box opens, click "Save", and select My Documents folder to download the file into. Save it under a file name that is relevant to the data and easy to remember. You may also create a new folder just for the downloaded data.

Click on this. When the download box opens, click "save", and select "My Docments" folder to save the file into. You may also create a new folder just for the downloaded data.

Mar-02	59.05	65.00	58.31	60.31	55,857,270	26.23
Feb-02	64.15	64.50	57.15	58.34	63,117,221	25.37
Jan-02	66.65	70.62	61.33	63.71	68,080,095	27.70
Dec-01	63.83	69.89	63.80	66.25	51,004,760	28.81
Nov-01	60.08	68.34	59.60	64.21	65,676,323	27.92
Oct-01	50.94	63.63	50.41	58.15	78,938,739	25.29
Sep-01	57.19	59.08	47.50	51.17	108,497,707	22.25
Aug-01	66.80	67.54	56.30	57.05	52,686,834	24.81
Jul-01	72.05	73.15	64.20	66.19	72,106,314	28.78
Jun-01	69.60	76.15	66.01	73.00	73,498,171	31.74
May-01	67.66	72.15	67.25	69.18	83,999,472	30.08
Apr-01	5.81	71.10	51.06	67.75	107,508,760	29.46
Mar-01	58.5	61.13	49.75	54.69	90,297,790	23.78
Feb-01	60.81	65.06	53.88	59.00	85,342,315	25.66
Jan-01	63.00	63.75	61.00	61.06	163,797,600	26.55

* Close price adjusted for dividends and splits.

First | Prev | **Next** | **Last**

Download To Spreadsheet

Now locate and open the downloaded file from the folder you saved it in. Once you open the file, highlight the column headings and delete all columns other than "Date" and "Adj. Close*" columns.

"Adj. Close*" means that it is the closing price adjusted for dividend payouts and stock splits. Since we are interested in finding the rate of return, let's apply what we have intuitively understood to the data available to us. As defined above, return is

$$r = \frac{\mathrm{Re}\textit{turn in \$}}{\mathrm{Pr}\textit{ice paid}} = \frac{\mathrm{Pr}\textit{ice @ po}\textrm{int } \textit{of sale} - \mathrm{Pr}\textit{ice @ po}\textrm{int } \textit{of purchase}}{\mathrm{Pr}\textit{ice @ po}\textrm{int } \textit{of purchase}} = \frac{P_t - P_{t-1}}{P_{t-1}}$$

where P_t is the price at current period,
P_{t-1} is the price at previous period.

So, if we rename the "Adj. Close" P_t, then P_{t-1} is the Adj. Close just one period prior. To facilitate the calculation we will copy column B from B3 all the way down into column C, we will have P_t and P_{t-1} next to each other.

	B3		Copy B.3	
	A	B	C	D	E
1	Date	Pt	Pt-1	rt	
2	3-Jul-06	22.48			
3	1-Jun-06	23.3			
4	1-May-06	22.65			
5	3-Apr-06	24.06			
6	1-Mar-06	27.1			
7	1-Feb-06	26.77			
8	3-Jan-06	27.95			
9	1-Dec-05	25.96			
10	1-Nov-05	27.48			

Highlight all the way down from B3, copy & paste it into C2.

	C2		= Paste		
	A	B	C	D	E
1	Date	Pt	Pt-1	rt	
2	3-Jul-06	22.48	23.3		
3	1-Jun-06	23.3	22.65		
4	1-May-06	22.65	24.06		
5	3-Apr-06	24.06	27.1		
6	1-Mar-06	27.1	26.77		
7	1-Feb-06	26.77	27.95		
8	3-Jan-06	27.95	25.96		
9	1-Dec-05	25.96	27.48		
10	1-Nov-05	27.48	25.44		

Now in cell D2, enter the equal sign (=) followed by the formula for return with each variable referring to the cell containing relevant data – *i.e.* B2 for P_t, and C2 for P_{t-1}. Pay attention to the use of parenthesis to avoid any error. Excel will execute multiplication and division before addition and subtraction by default, so without enclosing the numerator in the parenthesis, Excel will recognize only C2 as the numerator, and perform C2/C2 first and then subtract it from B2.

	STDEV		X ✓ = =(B2-C2)/C2	
	A	B	C	D	E
1	Date	P_t	P_{t-1}	r_t	
2	3-Jul-06	22.48	23.3	=(B2-C2)/C2	
3	1-Jun-06	23.3	22.65		
4	1-May-06	22.65	24.06		
5	3-Apr-06	24.06	27.1		
6	1-Mar-06	27.1	26.77		
7	1-Feb-06	26.77	27.95		
8	3-Jan-06	27.95	25.96		
9	1-Dec-05	25.96	27.48		
10	1-Nov-05	27.48	25.44		

Make sure the numerator is enclosed in parenthesis.

	STDEV		X ✓ = =(B2-C2)/C2	
	A	B	C	D	E
1	Date	P_t	Enter .1	r_t	
2	3-Jul-06	22.48	23.3	=(B2-C2)/C2	
3	1-Jun-06	23.3	22.65		
4	1-May-06	22.65	24.06		
5	3-Apr-06	24.06	27.1		
6	1-Mar-06	27.1	26.77		
7	1-Feb-06	26.77	27.95		
8	3-Jan-06	27.95	25.96		
9	1-Dec-05	25.96	27.48		
10	1-Nov-05	27.48	25.44		

Hit this green check mark to execute the formula entered.

The computed result will appear simply as a ratio, so we will need to convert it into %. It can easily be done by clicking on the % icon on the tool bar. You may also increase or decrease decimals, but we will set it to two places by convention.

Now that we have the monthly rate of return for June 1 through June 30 (July 3 in this example), we can copy and paste the formula over the entire data range to obtain monthly rate of return for each month.

Once we have these monthly returns, they can also serve us by providing the average of this trend of returns during the period in observation. This average can be used as an approximation of the return to be expected in the future. To find average, take the following steps.

First, locate the bottom of the returns data string. This is where the average of the returns will appear. Next to that cell, type in the descriptive label "Average". Then, click on *fx* (past function) icon on the toolbar to locate the Excel command "AVERAGE". You can also type it in the cell following an equal sign. (When you manually type it in, it doesn't matter whether you use upper case or lower case letters.)

Once you selected the desired command, then click "OK". Now, the following dialogue box will open up. It's merely asking you to enter the range of data that you wish to take the average of, so click on the spreadsheet icon in the first data window to highlight the data range into it. In our example it is N2 through N79, so if you highlight the exact range into it, Excel will automatically make it appear as follows. Then, hit "OK" and you will have the calculated average in the designated cell.

Stock Valuation Ratios

Valuation ratios are very useful tools for valuing stocks. There is a couple of ratios most commonly used, which are P/E ratio, PEG ratio and M/B ratio respectively.

a. P/E (Price/Earnings) Ratio

Also known as "earnings multiples", P/E ratio is used to measure how cheap or expensive its share prices is. The lower the P/E, the less you have to pay for the stock, relative to what you can expect to earn from it.

$$P/E \; ratio = \frac{\text{Pr} ice \; per \; share}{EPS}, \text{ where } EPS = \text{Earnings per share}$$

The price per share is the market price of a single share of the stock. The earnings per share is the EAT (earnings after taxes or net income or net profit all before dividend payout) divided by number of shares outstanding.

One most common misbelief in the stock market is that a high P/E ratio is an evidnece of a growth stock. It is allegedly due to the anticipated high and rapid growth, which is factored into price, pushing up the (often irrational) demand for the stock. Consequently, it is only pushing the price even further resulting in high P/E ratio regardless of the actual EPS. Also, this misbelief gets coupled with the seemingly plausible rationale that the fast growing firm uses all its available funds for expansion, leaving no room for earnings in the short run, which will be more than handsomely rewarded afterwards when the expansion is completed. However, nothing could be more grossly misguiding.

The P/E ratio certainly helps one to analyze the market's valuation of a firm's shares relative to the profit the firm actually generates, but not everyone understands that there are only two conditions, by its own mathematical construct, under which P/E can be high:

i) Both $\uparrow$P and $\uparrow$EPS are high, but the ΔP is far greater than the ΔEPS.
ii) $\uparrow$P is high while $\uparrow$EPS is minimal or none.

If it is i), there is no reason for concern. It is exactly the situation you want. However, if it is ii), then what drives P up is only the "irrational exuberance", and this is certainly not the ideal stock to hold no matter how high P/E is. For this reason, it is probably the most consistent signal to excessive optimism and over-investment.

One reason to calculate P/E is to compare the value of stocks within the same industry sector. If one stock has a P/E twice that of another, it is probably a less attractive investment. But comparisons between industries, between countries, and between time periods are misleading. For the P/E ratios to be meaningful, one should compare comparable stocks within the same industry. For examples, go straight to Figs II.B.1.a and II.B.1.b.

b. PEG (Price-Earnings-Growth) Ratio
The PEG ratio is a valuation metric that supplement the afore-mentioned shortcomings of P/E ratio. It compares the P/E against the earnings grwoth rate, which would justify the P/Es within the vicinity of the growth rate.

$$PEG\ ratio = \frac{P/E}{g}, \text{ where } g = \text{earnings growth rate.}$$

It is generally accepted that a PEG = 1 is an acceptable arbitrary bottom line. A lower ratio is better, because it means that the stock is cheaper for its growth, and a higher ratio is worse for the stock is expensive for its growth. It is not always clear whether the earnings used is the past year's EPS or the expected future EPS. It is always the expected future growth rate that is used.

PEG is more intuitively appealing, because it can offer a suggestion of whether a firm's high PE ratio reflects an excessively high stock price, or is a reflection of promising growth prospects for the firm. For this reason, it is a better measure than P/E ratio. However, the PEG ratio is less appropriate for measuring firms without high growth. Large, well-established firms, for instance, may offer dependable dividend income, but little opportunity for growth, but PEG does not offer much of such qualitative information as the firm's management.

c. M/B (Market Price/Book Value per Share) Ratio
Market-to-book ratio or M/B ratio, is used to compare a stock's market value to its book value. It is calculated by dividing the current closing price of the stock by the latest quarter's book value. Book value is the shareholders' equity (assets minus libilities) divided by the total number of outstanding shares.

$$M/B\ ratio = \frac{Market\ Price}{Book\ Value\ per\ Share}$$

A lower M/B ratio could mean that the stock is undervalued. However, it could also mean that something is fundamentally wrong with the firm. One caveat is that this ratio varies a fair amount by industry. Industries that require higher infrastructure capital, such as manufacturing or air lines, will usually trade at M/B much lower than the M/B of consulting firms for instance.

This ratio also gives some idea of whether one is paying too much for what would be left if the firm is forced into bankruptcy immediately. For examples, go straight to Figs II.B.1.a and II.B.1.b.

PROBLEM: Modify the above format accordingly and do Summary Practice Test problems 2 and 3.

Chapter 22 Problems

We will use problems 22-20 and 22-22. In problem 22-20, we will learn to create a bar graph (histogram) from the given data, and in problem 22-22, we will create a line graph from the given data. First, enter appropriate labels for each problem in column A. Column widths can be automatically adjusted by double-clicking on the border between column heads. Then, enter the data as shown below. To do this, we need Excel special feature called "Data Analysis" to be turned on. This feature is turned off in most low-level application, so if you don't see this function in the "Tools" menu as shown below, take the following steps.

First, select "Add-Ins", and when the dialogue box opens up, select "Analysis ToolPak" as shown below. You may also select "Solver Add-in" for future applications if it is not already selected. Once it is done, now you may notice that the data were entered at random. It will be nice if we sort this data in an ordered array – either descending or ascending. We can achieve this by selecting "Sort" in the "Data" menu in the toolbar.

	A	B				G
1	Customer $					
2	$ 18.50					
3	$ 18.24					
4	$ 16.10					
5	$ 12.11					
6	$ 15.88					
7	$ 3.55					
8	$ 3.82					
9	$ 3.95					
10	$ 6.88					
11	$ 14.10					
12	$ 2.10					
13	$ 5.50					
14	$ 9.95					
15	$ 6.80					

File Edit View Insert Format Tools Data Window Help

A1 ƒx Customer

Tools menu:
- Spelling... F7
- Research... Alt+Click
- Error Checking...
- Speech ▶
- Shared Workspace...
- Share Workbook...
- Track Changes ▶
- Compare and Merge Workbooks...
- Protection ▶
- Online Collaboration ▶
- Goal Seek...
- Scenarios...
- Formula Auditing ▶
- Solver...
- Macro ▶
- Add-Ins...
- AutoCorrect Options...
- Customize...
- Options...

Add-Ins [?][X]

Add-Ins available:
- ☑ Analysis ToolPak
- ☑ Analysis ToolPak - VBA
- ☐ Conditional Sum Wizard
- ☐ Euro Currency Tools
- ☐ Internet Assistant VBA
- ☐ Lookup Wizard
- ☑ Solver Add-in

OK
Cancel
Browse...
Automation...

Analysis ToolPak

Provides functions and interfaces for financial and scientific data analysis

Once you click on "Sort" in the menu box, a new dialogue box will open up. The sorting criteria is usually by the data labels, and since the "Customer $" (the amount each customer spent) is the only data label for now, and since we want to sort this data in descending order, we will select "Customer $", and check "Descending", and hit "OK". Also, make sure that you check the "Header row" since we have the data label in the first row.

	File	Edit	View	Insert	Format	Tools	Data	Window	Help		

A2 ▼ *fx* 18.5

	A	B	C							G
1	Customer $	Interval		Sort...						
2	$ 18.50			Filter ▶						
3	$ 18.24			Form...						
4	$ 16.10			Subtotals...						
5	$ 12.11			Validation...						
6	$ 15.88			Table...						
7	$ 3.55			Text to Columns...						
8	$ 3.82			Consolidate...						
9	$ 3.95			Group and Outline ▶						
10	$ 6.88			PivotTable and PivotChart Report...						
11	$ 14.10			Import External Data ▶						
12	$ 2.10			List ▶						
13	$ 5.50			XML ▶						
14	$ 9.95			Refresh Data						
15	$ 6.80									
16										

	A	B	C	D	E	F
1	Customer $					
2	$ 18.50		Sort			
3	$ 18.24					
4	$ 16.10		Sort by			
5	$ 12.11		Customer $ ▼	○ Ascending ⦿ Descending		
6	$ 15.88					
7	$ 3.55		Then by			
8	$ 3.82		▼	⦿ Ascending ○ Descending		
9	$ 3.95					
10	$ 6.88		Then by			
11	$ 14.10		▼	⦿ Ascending ○ Descending		
12	$ 2.10					
13	$ 5.50		My data range has			
14	$ 9.95		⦿ Header row ○ No header row			
15	$ 6.80					
16			Options... OK Cancel			

Now, we return to the "Data Analysis" in the "Tools" menu, and select "Histogram". Once the dialogue box opens up, we tell Excel where the data range for input is. We do it by the same manner as we have already done. Highlighting the data range and clicking it in by the spreadsheet icon in the corner of the data window. Next, we need to designate the "Bin Range".

	A	B	C	D	E	F	G
1	Customer $						
2	$ 18.50						
3	$ 18.24						
4	$ 16.10						
5	$ 12.11						
6	$ 15.88						
7	$ 3.55						
8	$ 3.82						
9	$ 3.95						
10	$ 6.88						
11	$ 14.10						
12	$ 2.10						
13	$ 5.50						
14	$ 9.95						
15	$ 6.80						
16							

Data Analysis

Analysis Tools

- Descriptive Statistics
- Exponential Smoothing
- F-Test Two-Sample for Variances
- Fourier Analysis
- Histogram
- Moving Average
- Random Number Generation
- Rank and Percentile
- Regression
- Sampling

OK   Cancel   Help

	A	B	C	D	E	F	G
1	Customer $	Interval					
2	$ 18.50	$ 23.99					
3	$ 18.24	$ 17.99					
4	$ 16.10	$ 11.99					
5	$ 15.88	$ 5.99					
6	$ 14.10						
7	$ 12.11						
8	$ 9.95						
9	$ 6.88						
10	$ 6.80						
11	$ 5.50						
12	$ 3.95						
13	$ 3.82						
14	$ 3.55						
15	$ 2.10						
16							
17							
18							
19							
20							
21							
22							

Histogram

Input

Input Range: $A$1:$A$15

Bin Range: $B$1:$B$5

☑ Labels

Output options

⦿ Output Range: $D$1

◯ New Worksheet Ply:

◯ New Workbook

☐ Pareto (sorted histogram)

☐ Cumulative Percentage

☐ Chart Output

OK   Cancel   Help

Bin is nothing but the intervals of data that will serve as bracket for each group of data. In our example, we already have a given intervals. We can enter only the upper bounds or the lower bounds only, because each upper bound will also serve as the lower bound for the next interval, and *vice versa*. Then, we will enter the "Bin Range" in the same manner as before. Make sure you check the "Labels" box, because the labels are included in the data range. Next, we will designate the "Output Range" to place the result in. We only need to select a single cell although the result will be a table. Excel will automatically take care of the rest. Now, hit "OK", and *voilà* the Frequency Distribution table!

While it is still highlighted, we will put a thick borderline around it by clicking the borderline icon in the toolbar. And while it is still highlighted, we will sort the table by interval in descending order.

	A	B	C	D	E	F
1	**Customer $**	**Interval**		*Interval*	*Frequency*	
2	$ 18.50	$ 23.99		5.99	5	
3	$ 18.24	$ 17.99		11.99	3	
4	$ 16.10	$ 11.99		17.99	4	
5	$ 15.88	$ 5.99		23.99	2	
6	$ 14.10			More	0	
7	$ 12.11					
8	$ 9.95					
9	$ 6.88					
10	$ 6.80					
11	$ 5.50					
12	$ 3.95					
13	$ 3.82					
14	$ 3.55					
15	$ 2.10					
16						

	A	B	C	D	E	F
1	**Customer $**	**Interval**		*Interval*	*Frequency*	
2	$ 18.50	$ 23.99		More	0	
3	$ 18.24	$ 17.99		23.99	2	
4	$ 16.10	$ 11.99		17.99	4	
5	$ 15.88	$ 5.99		11.99	3	
6	$ 14.10			5.99	5	
7	$ 12.11					
8	$ 9.95					
9	$ 6.88					
10	$ 6.80					
11	$ 5.50					
12	$ 3.95					
13	$ 3.82					
14	$ 3.55					
15	$ 2.10					
16						

D1   *fx* Interval   Chart Wizard

	A	B	C	D	E	F
1	**Customer $**	**Interval**		*Interval*	*Frequency*	
2	$ 18.50	$ 23.99		More	0	
3	$ 18.24	$ 17.99		23.99	2	
4	$ 16.10	$ 11.99		17.99	4	
5	$ 15.88	$ 5.99		11.99	3	
6	$ 14.10			5.99	5	
7	$ 12.11					
8	$ 9.95					
9	$ 6.88					
10	$ 6.80					
11	$ 5.50					
12	$ 3.95					
13	$ 3.82					
14	$ 3.55					
15	$ 2.10					
16						

Now, we are ready to generate a graph. First, locate the "Chart Wizard" icon from the toolbar as in the figure above and click on it while the table is still highlighted. (If the icon is not readily available, you can always bring it up by clicking on "Insert", "Picture", and "Chart" from the standard toolbar, or by clicking on "Tools", "Customize", "Command" and by locating the icon from the "Insert" menu.) A dialogue box will open up as in the figure below.

Since we want a bar graph, select the "Column" type in the left-side panel, and the available sub-types will appear in the right-side panel. You may pick any type you deem the best, but for our example, the ones in the middle row would do well since these types give 3-D effects. Pick one and then click on "Next". You will see a graph as in the figure below.

Keep in mind that this graph is based on the data in the highlighted table, so it would naturally contain two sets of data in the range – "Interval" and "Frequency". These data series are in columns (hence, you will see the "columns" checked in the dialogue box) of which the "Interval" is not the data we want to plot as vertical bar. It is actually the data to be plotted along the horizontal axis.

Therefore, we will click on the "Series" tab to modify the data series to be graphed. In the left-side panel you will see the two data series. The data series in columns are already highlighted. Just select the data string you want to remove, and hit "Remove" button. By the same token, you can also add new data series that you may also want to be on the graph.

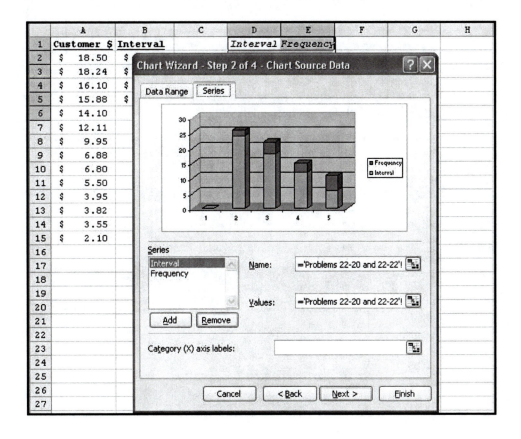

Now that we have only the data that we want to show as vertical bars, we will put the Interval data on the horizontal axis. Go to the "Category (X) axis labels:" at the bottom of the dialogue box and click on the icon in the right corner of the data window as indicated in the figure below.

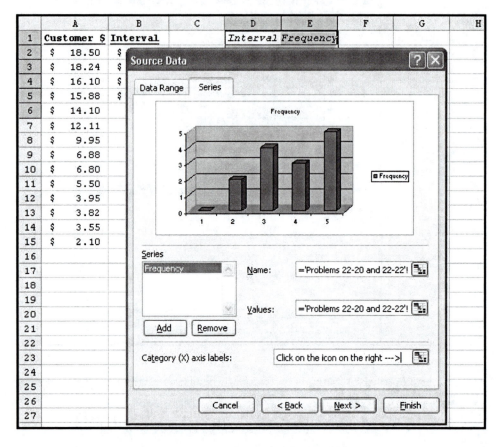

Once the data window opens, highlight only the range of intervals and click on the icon to enter it. Make sure that you don't include the label "Interval" in the data range.

	A	B	C	D	E	F	G
1	Customer $	Interval		Interval	Frequency		
2	$ 18.50	$ 23.99		More	0		
3	$ 18.24	$ 17.99		23.99	2		
4	$ 16.10	$ 11.99		17.99	4		
5	$ 15.88	$ 5.99		11.99	3		
6	$ 14.10			5.99	5		
7	$ 12.11						
8	$ 9.95						
9	$ 6.88						
10	$ 6.80						
11	$ 5.50						
12	$ 3.95						
13	$ 3.82						
14	$ 3.55						
15	$ 2.10						
16							

Source Data - Category (X) axis labels:

Highlight the range of intervals and click the icon in the right. ----->

	A	B	C	D	E	F	G
1	Customer $	Interval		Interval	Frequency		
2	$ 18.50	$ 23.99		More	0		
3	$ 18.24	$ 17.99		23.99	2		
4	$ 16.10	$ 11.99		17.99	4		
5	$ 15.88	$ 5.99		11.99	3		
6	$ 14.10			5.99	5		
7	$ 12.11						
8	$ 9.95						
9	$ 6.88						
10	$ 6.80						
11	$ 5.50						
12	$ 3.95						
13	$ 3.82						
14	$ 3.55						
15	$ 2.10						

Source Data - Category (X) axis labels:

='Problems 22-20 and 22-22'!$D$2:$D$6

If the data range is correctly entered, it will appear as in the following figure. Then, click on "Next".

Now, it's time to put the final details such as "chart title", "axis label"... etc. You may change the chart title to "Customer Spending Frequency" or whatever you think best describes the chart. You may also use whatever appropriate label for the horizontal axis. For our example, "Customer Spending Level" would be fine. And click "Next".

	A	B	C	D	E	F	G	H
1	Customer $	Interval			Interval Frequency			
2	$ 18.50							
3	$ 18.24							
4	$ 16.10							
5	$ 15.88							
6	$ 14.10							
7	$ 12.11							
8	$ 9.95							
9	$ 6.88							
10	$ 6.80							
11	$ 5.50							
12	$ 3.95							
13	$ 3.82							
14	$ 3.55							
15	$ 2.10							
16								
17								
18								
19								
20								

Chart Wizard - Step 3 of 4 - Chart Options

Titles | Axes | Gridlines | Legend | Data Labels | Data Table

Chart title:
Frequency

Category (X) axis:
Customer Spending

Series (Y) axis:

Value (Z) axis:

Cancel | < Back | Next > | Finish

Finally, we will decide where to place the chart. Normally, you would want to see the chart next to the data it represents. So, we will select the "As object in:" option to place it within the same worksheet as the data table. And click on "Finish". Once the chart is in place, you may move it around, modify and/or resize it for the desired visual effect.

By the same token, we can create the line graph with Problem 22-22, which we will skip in this exercise to avoid any redundancy.

	A	B	C	D	E	F	G	H
1	Customer $	Interval			Interval Frequency			
2	$ 18.50	$ 23.99		More	0			
3	$ 18.24	$ 17.99		23.99	2			
4	$ 16.10	$ 11.99		17.99	4			
5	$ 15.88	$ 5.99		11.99	3			
6	$ 14.10			5.99	5			
7	$ 12.11							
8	$ 9.95							
9	$ 6.88							
10	$ 6.80							
11	$ 5.50							
12	$ 3.95							
13	$ 3.82							
14	$ 3.55							
15	$ 2.10							
16								
17								
18								

Chart Wizard - Step 4 of 4 - Chart Location

Place chart:

○ As new sheet: Chart1

◉ As object in: Problems 22-20 and 22-22

Cancel | < Back | Next > | Finish

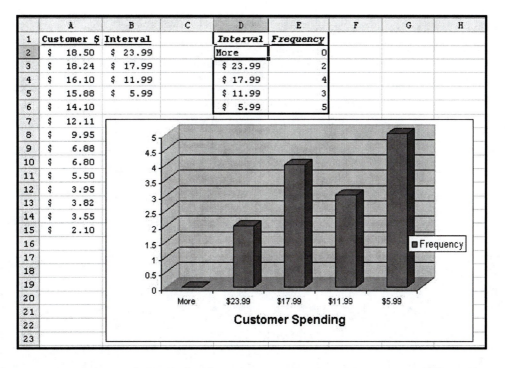

Now, let's turn our attention to the statistical issue in managing data. You may recall from Chapter 21 how we used Excel to find average. An average is a nice approximation, representative of a series of data. By its mathematical construct, however, an average of a long data series is an innocuous neutral number that doesn't capture the variation in data. To extend our example in Chapter 21, it is also of crucial importance for an investor to grasp the band of fluctuation in returns. However, it doesn't necessarily help the investor or a researcher to measure this band by the upper and lower bounds, because they don't happen all the time.

What a rational investor or research would need is only some approximation of average band of swings in the data (returns) – *i.e.* how much the data varies on average around the mean (average return). So, we need some metrics to capture this average range of variation in the data. There are largely two measures for doing this – variance and standard deviation, which are actually the same metrics in two outfits.

Now, let's review how we found average in Chapter 21. The following figures are the reproduction of what we have already seen in Chapter 21.

N2 = =(L2-M2)/M2

	K	L	M	N	O
1	Date	Pt	Pt-1	rt	
2	3-Jul-06	22.48	23.3	-3.52%	
3	1-Jun-06	23.3	22.65	2.87%	
4	1-May-06	22.65	24.06	-5.86%	
5	3-Apr-06	24.06	27.1	-11.22%	
6	1-Mar-06	27.1	26.77	1.23%	
7	1-Feb-06	26.77	27.95	-4.22%	
8	3-Jan-06	27.95	25.96	7.67%	
9	1-Dec-05	25.96	27.48	-5.53%	
10	1-Nov-05	27.48	25.44	8.02%	

AVERAGE = =AVERAGE(N2:N79)

	K	L	M	N	O
1	Date	Pt	Pt-1	rt	
71	2-Oct-00	29.95	26.23	14.18%	
72	1-Sep-00	26.23	30.36	-13.60%	
73	1-Aug-00	30.36	30.36	0.00%	
74	3-Jul-00	30.36	34.79	-12.73%	
75	1-Jun-00	34.79	27.2	27.90%	
76	1-May-00	27.2	30.33	-10.32%	
77	3-Apr-00	30.33	46.2	-34.35%	
78	1-Mar-00	46.2	38.86	18.89%	
79	1-Feb-00	38.86	42.56	-8.69%	
80	3-Jan-00		42.56	**Average** =AVERAGE(N2:N79)	

N80 | = |

	K	L	M	N	O
1	Date	Pt	Pt-1	rt	
70	1-Nov-00	24.95	29.95	-16.69%	
71	2-Oct-00	29.95	26.23	14.18%	
72	1-Sep-00	26.23	30.36	-13.60%	
73	1-Aug-00	30.36	30.36	0.00%	
74	3-Jul-00	30.36	34.79	-12.73%	
75	1-Jun-00	34.79	27.2	27.90%	
76	1-May-00	27.2	30.33	-10.32%	
77	3-Apr-00	30.33	46.2	-34.35%	
78	1-Mar-00	46.2	38.86	18.89%	
79	1-Feb-00	38.86	42.56	-8.69%	
80	3-Jan-00		42.56	**Average**	

Paste Function

Σ f* ᴢ↓ Create PDF Arial ▾ 11 ▾ **B** *I* U

N	O	P	Q	R	S	T	U
rt							

Paste Function ? ×

Function category: Function name:

Most Recently Used / All / Financial / Date & Time / Math & Trig / Statistical / Lookup & Reference / Database / Text / Logical / Information

AVERAGE / STDEV / SUM / IF / HYPERLINK / COUNT / MAX / SIN / SUMIF / PMT

AVERAGE(number1,number2,...)
Returns the average (arithmetic mean) of its arguments, which can be numbers or names, arrays, or references that contain numbers.

OK   Cancel

-16.69% / 14.18% / -13.60% / 0.00% / -12.73% / 27.90% / -10.32% / -34.35% / 18.89% / -8.69%

Microsoft Excel - msft

File Edit View Insert Format Tools Data Window Help

Σ f* ᴢ↓ » Create PDF

AVERAGE ▾ × ✓ = =AVERAGE(N2:N79)

AVERAGE

Number1 N2:N79 = {-0.0351931330472

Number2 = number

= -0.002301849

Returns the average (arithmetic mean) of its arguments, which can be numbers or names, arrays, or references that contain numbers.

Number1: number1,number2,... are 1 to 30 numeric arguments for which you want the average.

Formula result =-0.23%   OK   Cancel

We need another data series called the "difference terms", which we will label "$r_t - \bar{r}$", which literally means "return at time "t" – mean return", and thus the difference between individual returns and the average.

AVERAGE ▾ × ✓ = =D2-D$80

	A	B	C	D	E	F
1	Date	P_t	P_{t-1}	r_t	$r_t - \bar{r}$	
2	3-Jul-06	22.48	23.3	-3.52%	=D2-D$80	
3	1-Jun-06	23.3	22.65	2.87%		
4	1-May-06	22.65	24.06	-5.86%		
5	3-Apr-06	24.06	27.1	-11.22%		
6	1-Mar-06	27.1	26.77	1.23%		
7	1-Feb-06	26.77	27.95	-4.22%		
8	3-Jan-06	27.95	25.96	7.67%		
9	1-Dec-05	25.96	27.48	-5.53%		
10	1-Nov-05	27.48	25.44	8.02%		
11	3-Oct-05	25.44	25.47	-0.12%		
12	1-Sep-05	25.47	27.1	-6.01%		
13	1-Aug-05	27.1	25.28	7.20%		
14	1-Jul-05	25.28	24.52	3.10%		
15	1-Jun-05	24.52	25.46	-3.69%		

E2 ▾ = =D2-D$80

	A	B	C	D	E	F
1	Date	P_t	P_{t-1}	r_t	$r_t - \bar{r}$	
2	3-Jul-06	22.48	23.3	-3.52%	-3.29%	
3	1-Jun-06	23.3	22.65	2.87%	3.10%	
4	1-May-06	22.65	24.06	-5.86%	-5.63%	
5	3-Apr-06	24.06	27.1	-11.22%	-10.99%	
6	1-Mar-06	27.1	26.77	1.23%	1.46%	
7	1-Feb-06	26.77	27.95	-4.22%	-3.99%	
8	3-Jan-06	27.95	25.96	7.67%	7.90%	
9	1-Dec-05	25.96	27.48	-5.53%	-5.30%	
10	1-Nov-05	27.48	25.44	8.02%	8.25%	
11	3-Oct-05	25.44	25.47	-0.12%	0.11%	
12	1-Sep-05	25.47	27.1	-6.01%	-5.78%	
13	1-Aug-05	27.1	25.28	7.20%	7.43%	
14	1-Jul-05	25.28	24.52	3.10%	3.33%	
15	1-Jun-05	24.52	25.46	-3.69%	-3.46%	

Once you have found this term for the first row as in the figure above, the rest is just mechanical. All you have to do is just copy and paste it over the entire range below the first cell. Make sure that you have locked the cell containing the mean return (d80 as d$80 or d80 in the above example), so it can be copied without the hassle of adjusting for every row. Then, we will need another term called "difference squared" labeled "$(r_t - \bar{r})^2$", which is simply the square of the difference term. This term is there purely for technical reason, because if you sum all the difference terms, it will simply sum to zero. It is designed to be so by the very nature of the average and the difference term – *i.e.* the positive and negative difference terms will exactly offset each other. Then, the average of these difference terms will always be zero. So, it becomes inoperable to work with the difference terms. However, since squared terms of all real numbers are always positive, if we work with the squared terms, we won't have to worry about this problem.

AVERAGE		X ✓ =	=E2^2		
	A	B	C	D	E	F
1	Date	P_t	P_{t-1}	r_t	$r_t - \bar{r}$	$(r_t - \bar{r})^2$
2	3-Jul-06	22.48	23.3	-3.52%	-3.29%	=E2^2
3	1-Jun-06	23.3	22.65	2.87%	3.10%	
4	1-May-06	22.65	24.06	-5.86%	-5.63%	
5	3-Apr-06	24.06	27.1	-11.22%	-10.99%	
6	1-Mar-06	27.1	26.77	1.23%	1.46%	
7	1-Feb-06	26.77	27.95	-4.22%	-3.99%	
8	3-Jan-06	27.95	25.96	7.67%	7.90%	
9	1-Dec-05	25.96	27.48	-5.53%	-5.30%	
10	1-Nov-05	27.48	25.44	8.02%	8.25%	
11	3-Oct-05	25.44	25.47	-0.12%	0.11%	
12	1-Sep-05	25.47	27.1	-6.01%	-5.78%	
13	1-Aug-05	27.1	25.28	7.20%	7.43%	
14	1-Jul-05	25.28	24.52	3.10%	3.33%	
15	1-Jun-05	24.52	25.46	-3.69%	-3.46%	

F2		=	=E2^2		
	A	B	C	D	E	F
1	Date	P_t	P_{t-1}	r_t	$r_t - \bar{r}$	$(r_t - \bar{r})^2$
2	3-Jul-06	22.48	23.3	-3.52%	-3.29%	0.11%
3	1-Jun-06	23.3	22.65	2.87%	3.10%	0.10%
4	1-May-06	22.65	24.06	-5.86%	-5.63%	0.32%
5	3-Apr-06	24.06	27.1	-11.22%	-10.99%	1.21%
6	1-Mar-06	27.1	26.77	1.23%	1.46%	0.02%
7	1-Feb-06	26.77	27.95	-4.22%	-3.99%	0.16%
8	3-Jan-06	27.95	25.96	7.67%	7.90%	0.62%
9	1-Dec-05	25.96	27.48	-5.53%	-5.30%	0.28%
10	1-Nov-05	27.48	25.44	8.02%	8.25%	0.68%
11	3-Oct-05	25.44	25.47	-0.12%	0.11%	0.00%
12	1-Sep-05	25.47	27.1	-6.01%	-5.78%	0.33%
13	1-Aug-05	27.1	25.28	7.20%	7.43%	0.55%
14	1-Jul-05	25.28	24.52	3.10%	3.33%	0.11%
15	1-Jun-05	24.52	25.46	-3.69%	-3.46%	0.12%

So, we will simply raise the difference term in e2 to the 2nd power as in the figure above, and copy and paste it all the way down. Once you have all the squared difference terms, you will need to sum them up in order to find an average. This summed result is call "sum of squares (SSQ)". Once we have SSQ, then we need to divide it by the "number of observations – 1". (This is due to an important statistical factor called degree of freedom.)

F80		=		AutoSum	
	A	B	C	D	E	F
1	Date	P_t	P_{t-1}	r_t	$r_t - \bar{r}$	$(r_t - \bar{r})^2$
70	1-Nov-00	**Sum of Squares**		9%	-16.46%	2.71%
71	2-Oct-00			8%	14.41%	2.08%
72	1-Sep-00	26.23	30.36	-13.60%	-13.37%	1.79%
73	1-Aug-00	30.36	30.36	0.00%	0.23%	0.00%
74	3-Jul-00	30.36	34.79	-12.73%	-12.50%	1.56%
75	1-Jun-00	34.79	27.2	27.90%	28.13%	7.92%
76	1-May-00	27.2	30.33	-10.32%	-10.09%	1.02%
77	3-Apr-00	30.33	46.2	-34.35%	-34.12%	11.64%
78	1-Mar-00	46.2	38.86	18.89%	19.12%	3.66%
79	1-Feb-00	38.86	42.56	-8.69%	.46%	0.72%
80	3-Jan-00	42.56	Average	-0.23%	SSQ	

AVERAGE		X ✓ =	=SUM(F2:F79)			
	A	B	C	D	E	F	G
1	Date	P_t	P_{t-1}	r_t	$r_t - \bar{r}$	$(r_t - \bar{r})^2$	
70	1-Nov-00	24.95	29.95	-16.69%	-16.46%	2.71%	
71	2-Oct-00	29.95	26.23	14.18%	14.41%	2.08%	
72	1-Sep-00	26.23	30.36	-13.60%	-13.37%	1.79%	
73	1-Aug-00	30.36	30.36	0.00%	0.23%	0.00%	
74	3-Jul-00	30.36	34.79	-12.73%	-12.50%	1.56%	
75	1-Jun-00	34.79	27.2	27.90%	28.13%	7.92%	
76	1-May-00	27.2	30.33	-10.32%	-10.09%	1.02%	
77	3-Apr-00	30.33	46.2	-34.35%	-34.12%	11.64%	
78	1-Mar-00	46.2	38.86	18.89%	19.12%	3.66%	
79	1-Feb-00	38.86	42.56	-8.69%	-8.46%	0.72%	
80	3-Jan-00	42.56	Average	-0.23%	SSQ	=SUM(F2:F79)	

The result is called the (sample) "variance", which is expressed mathematically as $VAR(r) = \dfrac{\sum\limits_{t=1}^{n}(r_t - r)^2}{n-1}$,

meaning that the variance of returns (r) is the approximate average of all the SSQ's, where number of observation runs from 1 to n. Statistically, we need to distinguish between sample variance and population variance, where population variance is the average of all the SSQ's, where number of

observation runs from 1 to n. Mathematically, it is expressed as $\sigma_r^2 = \dfrac{\sum_{t=1}^{n}(r_t - r)^2}{n}$, of which the

interpretation is pretty much the same as the sample variance above. The only difference, however, is that the latter uses n, not $n-1$, in the denominator. We won't dwell on the theoretical background for this difference, as a course in statistics will well expound it, and thus, focus mainly on the practical implication for large samples. Theoretically, as the n reaches infinity, the difference between n and $n-1$ will be insignificant. Practically, as the sample size "n" increases, the difference between the two also becomes meaningless as long as we have a decent-size sample[13] with normal distribution.

We can also find the variance using Excel's built-in command. The procedure is the same as in finding average. Locate the *fx* icon in the toolbar or the formula window (The location of the *fx* icon varies by Excel version.). When the "Paste Function" dialogue box opens up, look for "VAR". If you don't see it from the list of "Most Recently Used" functions, then go to "All functions", and select "Statistical" in the

---

[13] In general, a sample with more than 30 observations is considered to exhibit characteristics of normal distribution.

left-side panel. Then locate "VAR" and click on it. A data window will open up. Click on the spreadsheet icon in the right corner, highlight and enter the data series you want to find the variance of.

In our example, we want to find the variance of the monthly returns data series. So, we enter the data range f2 through f79 as shown in the figure above. Once done, hit "O.K." and *voilà* the variance! (If you used the same data, you would get 1.2% either by dividing SSQ by 77 ($n-1$) or by using Excel's VAR command.)

Now that the variance is found, we have found the approximated average variation of the returns around the mean, or have we not? Yes, and not quite yet. One thing we need to remember is that the variance is based on squared difference terms, remember? – *i.e.* we had to square all difference terms to avoid summing up to zero. So, the variance isn't quite the life-size picture of the average variation, but rather a blown-up picture of it. Therefore, we need to revert it back to its original size. And since the original self of the squared terms is the square root of them, all we need to do is to simply take the square root of the variance to revert it back to its original self. This is called the "standard deviation" (STDEV).

Mathematically it is defined as $Stdev(r) = \sqrt{\dfrac{\sum_{t=1}^{n}(r_t - \bar{r})^2}{n-1}}$ for sample, or $\delta = \sqrt{\dfrac{\sum_{t=1}^{n}(r_t - \bar{r})^2}{n}}$ for population.

Compare these formulas with those of the variance. The relationship between the two is quite self-explanatory. Especially, the relationship between symbol for population variance (σ^2) and population standard deviation (σ) is quite illustrative.

In order to find standard deviation, we can simply use Excel command "=SQRT(cell # of the variance)" next to the variance, and label it "Stdev", or just look for the STDEV command from Excel's *fx* ("Paste Function") feature, and highlight and enter the data series to find the standard deviation of.

	D81		f_x =STDEV(E2:E79)			
	A	C	D	E	F	G
1	Date	P_{t+1}	r_t	$r_t \quad -$	$(r_t \quad - \quad \bar{r})^2$	
70	36831	29.95	=(B70-C70)/C70	=D70-D$80	=E70^2	
71	36801	26.23	=(B71-C71)/C71	=D71-D$80	=E71^2	
72	36770	30.36	=(B72-C72)/C72	=D72-D$80	=E72^2	
73	36739	30.36	=(B73-C73)/C73	=D73-D$80	=E73^2	
74	36710	34.79	=(B74-C74)/C74	=D74-D$80	=E74^2	
75	36678	27.2	=(B75-C75)/C75	=D75-D$80	=E75^2	
76	36647	30.33	=(B76-C76)/C76	=D76-D$80	=E76^2	
77	36619	46.2	=(B77-C77)/C77	=D77-D$80	=E77^2	
78	36586	38.86	=(B78-C78)/C78	=D78-D$80	=E78^2	
79	36557	42.56	=(B79-C79)/C79	=D79-D$80	=E79^2	
80	36528	Average	=AVERAGE(D2:D79)	SSQ	=SUM(F2:F79)	
81		Stdev	=STDEV(E2:E79)	VAR	=VAR(E2:E79)	
82		Stdev	=SQRT(F82)	VAR	=F80/(78-1)	
83						

PROBLEM: Apply the above procedures to do Challenge Problems 22-23.

Appendix A: *FORMULAS FOR PROBLEMS*

CHAPTER 4

CELL B14	=B3+B5-B7-B9-B11
CELL E14	=E3+E5-E9-E10-E11

CHAPTER 6

CELL B7	=B3-B5
CELL C5	=B5/B3
CELL C7	=B7/B3

CHAPTER 7

CELL A5	=1.00-A3
CELL B5	=1.00-B3
CELL D5	=1.00-D3
CELL E5	=1.00-E3
CELL B7	=1.000-A5*B5
CELL E7	=1.000-D5*E5

CHAPTER 8

CELL B3	=A3*.80
CELL C3	=B3*.90
CELL D3	=C3*1.12
CELL E3	=D3*.95
CELL F3	=(A3-E3)/A3

CHAPTER 9

CELL C7	=C3*C5
CELL C13	=C9*C11
CELL C15	=C7+C13

CHAPTER 10

CELL E2	=D2-C2
CELL F2	=A2*B2*E2/360
CELL G2	=A2+F2
PROBLEM: CHANGE CELL F2 for 365 days	
CELL F2	=A2*B2*E2/365

CHAPTER 11

CELL B4	=B1*B2*(B3/360)
CELL B5	=B1-B4
CELL B6	+B1
CELL B7	=B4/((B5*(B3/360))

CHAPTER 12

PROBLEM 12-7:

CELL E2	=B2*2
CELL F2	=C2/2
CELL H2	=A2*G2

PROBLEM 12-8:

CELL E2	=B2*12
CELL F2	=C2/12

PROBLEM 12-9:

CELL E2	=B2*4
CELL F2	=C2/4

PROBLEM 12-10:

CELL E2	=B2*1
CELL F2	=C2/1

CHAPTER 13

CELL C2	=A5/4
CELL C4	=A7*4
CELL E2	=A3*D2

CHAPTER 14

CELL D1	=B1-B4
CELL D2	=(B3*B2)-D1

CHAPTER 15

CELL C2	=A2-B2
CELL G2	=C2/1000*F2

CHAPTER 16

CELL B7	=SUM(B3:B6)
CELL B11	=B9+B10
CELL B12	=B7+B11
CELL B17	=B15+B16
CELL B20	=B17+B19
CELL B23	=B20+B22
CELL C7	=SUM(C3:C6)
CELL C11	=C9+C10
CELL C12	=C7+C11
CELL C17	=C15+C16
CELL C20	=C17+C19
CELL C23	=C20+C22

CELL D3	=B3-C3
CELL D4	=B4-C4
CELL D5	=B5-C5
CELL D6	=B6-C6
CELL D7	=B7-C7
CELL D9	=B9-C9
CELL D10	=B10-C10
CELL D11	=B11-C11
CELL D12	=B12-C12
CELL D15	=B15-C15
CELL D16	=B16-C16
CELL D17	=B17-C17
CELL D19	=B19-C19
CELL D20	=B20-C20
CELL D22	=B22-C22
CELL D23	=B23-C23
CELL E3	=D3/C3
CELL E4	=D4/C4
CELL E5	=D5/C5
CELL E6	=D6/C6
CELL E7	=D7/C7
CELL E9	=D9/C9
CELL E10	=D10/C10
CELL E11	=D11/C11
CELL E12	=D12/C12
CELL E15	=D15/C15
CELL E16	=D16/C16
CELL E17	=D17/C17
CELL E19	=D19/C19
CELL E20	=D20/C20
CELL E22	=D22/C22
CELL E23	=D23/C23

CHAPTER 17

CELL B6	=(B1-B3)/B2*B4
CELL B7	=B1-B6
CELL B8	=B7-B5

CHAPTER 18

CELL B6	=B4*B5
CELL B11	=B9*B10
CELL B16	=B14*B15
CELL B18	=B6+B11+B16
CELL B20	=(B4*B5)+(B19-B46)*B10
CELL B21	=B18-B20

CHAPTER 19

CELL C6	=C4/C5
CELL C10	=C8*C9
CELL C12	=C10*C11

CHAPTER 20

PROBLEM 20-8:

CELL D8	=C9*D6
CELL D9	=C9*D7
CELL D10	=SUM(D8:D9)

PROBLEM 20-9:

CELL C15	=C13*D14
CELL C16	=C13-C15

PROBLEM 20-11:

CELL C20	=C19*D20
CELL C23	=C22*D23
CELL D23	=C21/C20

CHAPTER 21

PROBLEM 21-19

CELL B8	=B6/B5
CELL B9	=B7/B6

CHAPTER 22

APPENDIX B: *Examples and Problems*

Using Excel Templates for Problems and Examples

The Excel spreadsheets included in this package are designed to work with Practical Business Math Procedures (8e) by Jeffrey Slater. There is one exercise per chapter which demonstrates a particular lesson within that chapter. In addition, there are two problems for each chapter taken from the problems section at the end of the chapter. Students are encouraged to make a copy of the entire disk and use it in the lab or at home.

A knowledge of Excel would be helpful in doing the problems but it is not essential. Students place data in the **yellow** cells and the formulas will automatically calculate. Do not be concerned with the how the spreadsheet looks on the screen.

Students who are familiar with Excel will note that each of the Chapter Exercises contains the letters "EX" followed by the chapter it is found in (i.e. EX1, Ex2, etc.). The same is true of the Chapter Problems (i.e. Chpt.01, Chapt.02, etc.) There also is the extension .XLS. Accessing these files is through the OPEN command and students can open as many chapters as they wish. It is not necessary to close each chapter file in order to open the next chapter file.

General Instructions

Each Excel template is designed the same way. The problems are numbered to match the problem numbers at the end of each chapter. The exercises are numbered to match the chapter the exercise can be found. Number and title identify each problem on the screen. Please follow these steps:

Step 1: You may use the files from the disk/CD or transfer them to the your hard drive. Most college labs will not allow students to transfer the files to the lab hard drive. If you are able to transfer the files to your own disk/CD, follow the instructions for copying the files.

Step 2: If Excel is part of the Microsoft Office, double click on that work group to open it.

Step 3: Double click on the Excel icon. Your version of Excel may look different than the screens printed in the workbook. All the problems and exercises work with any version of Excel.

With the Excel program loaded, you are now ready to start your work. Each time you will use the FILE pull down menu, click on that menu once, and then you will use the OPEN command, again with one click. Now you may choose the chapter or the example you wish. Each chapter is headed by the letters CHPT. and followed by the chapter number. Each exercise is headed by the letters EX and followed by the chapter number. You may disregard the file extension .XLS. If you wish chapter one you would place the mouse arrow on CHPT.01.XLS and click twice. If you wish the example you would place the mouse arrow on EX1.XLS and click twice.

When you are ready to move on to another chapter or exercise, you again select the FILE pull down menu, click once, and then select OPEN and click once. You may open as many chapters and/ or examples as you wish. When done you can close any chapter and/or example by selecting FILE pull down menu, click once, and then select CLOSE and click once.

You will also note that you may do the chapters and/or the exercises in any order you wish. If you save your work, use the **SAVE AS** feature and use a different name for your work files. Later, you can open those files.

There is a conversion table file, named TABLES.XLS for doing some of the math conversion work for you. This table will find compound interest, present value, amount of annuity, present value of annuity, sinking fund, and amortization. You enter the interest rate and the time. The table is rounded off after four (4) decimal places. There is no limit on the interest rate or the number of years.

Using A Floppy Disk or CD Drive

If you use a floppy disk or CD drive it will be necessary for you to change the disk drive when you use the FILE - OPEN method of retrieving your files. After placing the floppy disk in your disk drive, or CD in CD drive, select FILE pull down menu and click once. Then select the OPEN command and click once. Now you will have to change the disk drive by using the DISK DRIVE selection box arrow beside the "MY DOCUMENTS" title. You would place the mouse arrow on the arrow and click once. A series of choices, starting with A: for the A drive will appear. Select the proper drive letter and click. That will switch the disk drive or CD drive. Now return to the FILENAME listings, select the chapter, click twice and the file will load.

Using Excel Without The Mouse

If you do not have a mouse, or if the mouse is not working, you can use Excel through the keyboard. To select the FILE pull down menu, press the ALT key on either side of the space bar. The FILE pull down menu name will be highlighted. Press the ENTER key and it will open. Using the DOWN ARROW key you can highlight the OPEN command. Again press ENTER. Now you can type, from the keyboard, the chapter you wish and press ENTER and the file will load. Check your Excel manual for additional keys and how they work.

Instructions On Screen

Each **exercise** contains information and yellow cells for the information you will find in the lesson in the book.

Each **chapter** file has two problems from the book. Only one is on screen. In order to move to the other problem follow the instructions at the bottom of the screen. You need only click on the sheet name at the bottom of the spreadsheet to go from one sheet to the other. You may change sheets without loosing data.

The spreadsheets are locked so you cannot accidentally put information into the wrong cell.

Disk Directory for Examples

FILENAME	CHAPTER LESSON
Ex1	Converting to a Whole Number
Ex2	Working with Fractions
Ex3	Rounding to Tenths, Hundreds, Thousands
Ex4	Format of a Check
Ex5	Solving Equations
Ex6	Converting Decimals and Percents
Ex7	Trade Discount, Net Price, Complement of Trade Discount
Ex8	Calculating Dollar and Percent Markup
Ex9	Calculating Employee's Pay, Including Overtime
Ex10	Calculating Simple Interest and Maturity Rate
Ex11	Discounting Interest-Bearing Note Before Maturity
Ex12	Simple vs. Compound Interest
Ex13	Calculating Present Value
Ex14	Cost of Installment Buying
Ex15	Calculating Interest Over the Life of a Mortgage
Ex16	Calculating Net Sales, Cost of Merchandise Sold, Gross Profit, Net Income
Ex17	Straight Line Method of Depreciation
Ex18	Retail and Gross Profit Method for Inventory
Ex19	Calculating Sales and Excise Tax
Ex20	Calculating Fire, Life, and Auto Insurance
Ex21	Calculating Return of Investment
Ex22	Calculating Mean, Median, and Mode

Disk Directory For Problems

FILENAME	CHAPTER TITLE IN BOOK
CHPT.01	Whole Numbers
CHPT.02	Fractions
CHPT.03	Decimals
CHPT.04	Banking
CHPT.05	Solving For The Unknown
CHPT.06	Percents and Their Applications
CHPT.07	Discounts: Trade and Cash
CHPT.08	Markups and Markdowns; Insight into Perishables
CHPT.09	Payroll
CHPT.10	Simple Interest
CHPT.11	Promissory Notes, Simple Discount Notes, and the Discount Process
CHPT.12	Compound Interest and Present Value
CHPT.13	Annuities and Sinking Funds
CHPT.14	Installment Buying, Rule of 78, and Revolving Charge Credit Cards
CHPT.15	The Cost of Home Ownership
CHPT.16	How to Read, Analyze, and Interpret Financial Reports
CHPT.17	Depreciation
CHPT.18	Inventory and Overhead
CHPT.19	Sales, Excise, and Property Tax
CHPT.20	Life, Fire, and Auto Insurance
CHPT.21	Stocks, Bonds, and Mutual Funds
CHPT.22	Business Statistics
TABLE	Table to Calculate Compounded Interest, Present Value, Amount of Annuity, Present Value of Annuity, Sinking Fund, Amortization